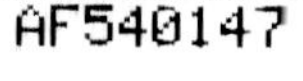

Nĩti

TIMELESS INDIAN WISDOM ON BUSINESS SUCCESS, WEALTH & POWER

Nĩti

Timeless Indian
Wisdom on Business Success,
Wealth & Power

ASHU DUTT | ANAV DUTT

www.visionbooksindia.com

www.visionbooksindia.com

A Vision Books Original

ISBN 10: 81-7094-966-1
ISBN 13: 978-81-7094-966-4

First Published in 2016
by
Vision Books Pvt. Ltd.
(Incorporating Orient Paperbacks and CARING imprints)
24 Feroze Gandhi Road, Lajpat Nagar 3
New Delhi 110024, India.
Phone: (+91-11) 2984 0821 / 22
e-mail: visionbooks@gmail.com

Printed at
Anand Sons
C 88, Ganesh Nagar, Pandav Nagar Complex
Delhi 110092, India.

Dedication

~

To my children,
Arshiya Dutt and Ahren Dutt.
You are the motivation
for all my works!

Contents

Introduction

"Like us many have spoken over this spring,
But they were gone in a twinkling of an eye,
We conquered the world with bravery and might
But we did not take it to our graves.'
— *Baburnama*

I got interested in writings on Indian wisdom when I first chanced upon the *Panchtantra*. As I read more, I realized their tremendous potential to influence and help companies and businesses — and the professionals who worked in the corporates and ran them. Moreover, I found their application was universal. Having spent my life around the globe, with substantial time periods in the US and India, worked in senior management at a very young age in both these countries, and having gone to college in the US, I realized that their wisdom would interest a global audience. Many of my colleagues in the US had read Japanese- and Chinese-based works on winning, strategy and governance, but rarely a work from India.

Once I set out on it, I found other texts from India which contained riches of timeless wisdom on power, fortune and success. There were a few issues though that could keep this wisdom from contemporary Indian and global audience. These were:

- Most of the available translations were "literal" translations, usually written by academics. Consequently, they failed to sufficiently etch out the underlying management and governance message.
- The language was cumbersome and sometimes required an "Indian" or an "Indian's" perspective or some awareness of India's culture or surroundings to understand.
- There was no single body of work that had mined and gathered together such material from a cross section of the available texts and sources.

I wanted to put these writings in a format that the corporate and business world, administrators and professionals would understand and profit from. To do so, Anav and I had to often abridge many of the extracts to make them accessible even for those without a background of Indian culture or nuances. We also worked on the language to make it more universal and kept in perspective the mindset of the contemporary global professional who has read lots of books on motivation, strategy, and management techniques.

I hope you will like this work and benefit from it. The book is the result of our effort to unearth thousands of years of Indian wisdom on success, wealth and power.

ASHU DUTT

Action

Fools limit knowledge to the books;
wise men put knowledge into action.
Ointments heal wounds only when they are applied
and not by their mere mention.

— *Panchtantra*

It's fortune's loss if it fights shy of a man who is brave, wise, discreet, diligent, enterprising; and who is not mean, wayward or disloyal.

— *Panchtantra*

Counsel makes a difference if it is put into action.
Mere knowledge of the solution never cured a problem.

— *Hitopadeśa*

Just like a lamp provides no light in a blind man's hand, the rules of science will not benefit those who don't apply them.

— *Hitopadeśa*

Men who speak with indecision, or those who don't persevere, or those who blame a hundred stumbling blocks at each step, are bound to sound hollow when their enterprise turns out to be a disappointment, turning such men into a laughing stock.

— *Panchtantra*

Any enterprise not done in time will not succeed,
especially the one that is sure to bear fruit.
— *Panchtantra*

A ship, to cross the fearful seas,
a lamp, to dispel the darkeness,
a fan, to make up for the lack of breeze,
a goad to move an unwilling elephant;
there's nothing in the world,
for which there isn't a cure.
— *Hitopadeśa*

Only when tasks undertaken are completed, can activity be considered fruitful.
— Chanakya

By his action a man goes
to great heights or sinks deep.
Just like someone who builds a tall tower,
or digs a mine deep.
— *Hitopadeśa*

Not starting, because we fear failure
is a sure sign of failure.
Do we stop eating
just because we fear getting a stomach ache?
— *Hitopadeśa*

Fear danger when it is at a distance.
But once it is imminent, strike with a hero's zest.

— *Hitopadeśa*

Seize opportunities or you will run into obstacles.

— Chanakya

It is not possible for a person with only theoretical knowledge and no practical know — how to accomplish any tasks.

— Chanakya

Don't brag if you cannot deliver.
Like thundering clouds with no rain,
the wise don't brag about what they are capable of.

— *Hitopadeśa*

If you don't take or give when it is due,
or do something when it needs to be done,
its time and essence are gone.

— *Hitopadeśa*

The power to make things possible is yours.
Put your plans into action with this thought,
and your plans will bear fruit.

— *Panchtantra*

Why blame destiny when adversity may be a result of our own actions.

— *Hitopadeśa*

Just as the best medicine has to be taken to cure a patient; ignorance cannot be removed without putting learning to practice.

— *Hitopadeśa*

Fate is nothing but a fruit of your actions. So get rid of laziness, change your habits to strive with all your strength.

— *Hitopadeśa*

Fate won't pick up a diamond lying in the rubble and hand it over to you. You have to take that trouble.

— *Hitopadeśa*

Go to battle ready for death
when it seems futile to withdraw.

— *Hitopadeśa*

No burden is too great,
for those with strong and able minds.
No destination is too far,
for those who are enterprising.
No country is a foreign land,
for those who have the knowledge.

— *Hitopadeśa*

Alliances

They clasp your hands to greet you.
Their eyes are misty with affection.
They give up their seat to allow you to sit.
They listen tirelessly to you and make pleasant talk.
Be careful of such people.
They are adept at deceit and tricks;
honey on the top and poison hidden deep within.

— *Panchtantra*

Alliances formed or based on money, or a position in an organization, will not hold. They collapse with the loss of money or position.

— Chanakya

Melting brings metals together.
Nature brings animals together.
Greed and fear brings foolish men together.
And perceptions bring the noble together.

— *Hitopadeśa*

You can only shine in the company of the great.
Just as the grass on the hillside grows by its nearness to the sun.

— *Hitopadeśa*

The following are the categories of kings with whom it is difficult to conclude an alliance; even when one is concluded, they quickly become dissatisfied:

- One who has attacked an ally either by joining force with or under the influence of others;
- One who has deserted an alliance for the sake of another or due to weakness or greed;
- One who has sold himself for a price to the enemy and has withdrawn himself from fighting for alliance;
- One who, after agreeing to the dual policy of making peace with one and attacking another, goes off in some other direction and attacks another enemy and not the one agreed upon;
- One who, having inspired confidence in an ally, joins a different expedition or undertakes an expedition on his own;
- One who does not come to his ally's help in times of calamities due to fear, contempt or laziness;
- One who is forcibly kept out of his own place or has left his country out of fear;
- One who has been humiliated by having his possession snatched away, by being refused what is due to him or by being given unwelcome things;
- One who has been forced to pay tribute or who voluntarily pays an excessive tribute;
- One who goes over to the enemy;
- One who has been ignored, having been earlier considered weak; or
- One who ignores requests for an alliance

— *Arthaśāstra*

Unheated metal does not mix with metal.
The essence of alliances is power.

— Chanakya

Before entering into an alliance, make sure you have complete information on the person's conduct and strength.

— *Panchtantra*

When you are rich, all men are your friends;
But in a crisis, only a true friend stands by you.

— *Panchtantra*

A friend is defined by these five properties:

- he can keep secrets;
- he speaks the truth;
- he controls his anger;
- he avoids gambling; and
- he remains a friend in bad times.

— *Hitopadeśa*

Prosperity changes loyalties.
An ally with increased power cannot be trusted.

— Chanakya

Relationships that are based on fine manners, extravagant courtesies, compliments and praise, are sure to turn into loathing, disdain and dishonor at some point.

— *Panchtantra*

Marriages and friendship work well between those with similar wealth and lineage profiles. Not between the well bred and prosperous and the lean and poor.

— *Panchtantra*

A risky acquisition is one which carries the danger of a risk in the future. A wrong acquisition is one which provokes either an internal rebellion or external wrath.

— *Arthaśāstra*

Aggressors are of three types-the righteous aggressor who only wants submission, the greedy aggressor who wants land and goods, and the monstrous aggressor who, on top of seizing land, goods, wives and sons, is satisfied only by taking the life of his victim.

— *Arthaśāstra*

The only way to maintain an alliance is to make sure the terms of the agreement are not fulfilled in full measure. There can be no alliance with people who are satisfied or with those whose terms have been met.

— Chanakya

Ambition

Like wild flowers,
the ambitious have two courses in life.
To be successful and get noticed
or wither into oblivion.

— *Hitopadeśa*

There are six qualities that hinder growth:

- Surrendering to feminine grace;
- Being partial to friends and family;
- Being lazy, sickly or diffident;
- And being content with what you already have.

— *Hitopadeśa*

Everything is fine in life till you don't trip.
But once you begin to stumble,
every step becomes painful.

— *Panchtantra*

If you believe destiny drives success or adversity, then you are going to end up doing nothing.

— *Hitopadeśa*

You can obtain and attain anything if you try,
and that's what I shall now set out and do.

— *Panchtantra*

The right opportunity comes once
for those who wait eagerly.
'Tis not easy to find another opportunity
to do what you wish to.

— Panchtantra

For the strong and able,
no effort is too much.
For the enterprising,
no destination is too far.
For those with knowledge,
no country is a foreign land.
For those with gentleness, none is an enemy.

— Hitopadeśa

The ocean cannot quench its own thirst.

— Chanakya

Don't be straightforward.
Straight trees are cut down
and crooked ones left standing in the forest.

— Chanakya

A ruler should never be satisfied
with the revenues he receives;
much as an ocean is never satisfied
by the rivers that drain into it,
or a scholar with the knowledge he acquires,
or a person in love
with the mere sight of the one he loves.

— Chanakya

I have drunk foul water.
I have slept on grass.
I have endured parting from those I love.
I have winced but spoken humbly to strangers.
I have trudged roads and crossed seas.
Is there anything else you want me to do, Desire?
For God's sake, say it — and be done!

— *Panchtantra*

Men fight for fame or honour,
rarely for money alone.

— *Hitopadeśa*

There is the prospect of impossibility when ambitious men want what they cannot get. That holds true for children and pretty women, and those made vain by wealth — and the insane.

— *Hitopadeśa*

There is no man without desire.

— Chanakya

Ambitious men choose national service to pursue their ambition. That's the real reason for their serving in the government, for they can earn a living anywhere.

— *Hitopadeśa*

Lions, elephants and enterprising men,
leave their homes and go far.
Only cowards, crows and deer
stay in the same place till death.

— *Hitopadeśa*

For men with courage and ambition,
no place is home or foreign.
Wherever they go, they will make it their own.

— *Hitopadeśa*

As frogs find a home in wells and ponds,
and storks in lakes,
fortune finds a home in enterprising men.

— *Hitopadeśa*

Laziness, indulgence, diffidence, anger and procrastination are the five faults to avoid if you want to succeed.

— *Hitopadeśa*

Nothing is impossible
if you have the intelligence.
Nothing is unachievable if you have the will.
Nothing is unattainable if you persevere.

— *Panchtantra*

Canal makers lead the water wherever they like.
Archers send the arrow to the target they like.
Carpenters bend a log of wood to the shape they like.
Wise men fashion their destiny the way they like.

— *Sutta Pitaka*

A man with a passion for honour and ambition cannot rest content with an unrealized dream.

— *Panchtantra*

There is no space for peace in the heart of a man filled with bursting ambition.

— *Panchtantra*

An ambitious man bides his time even if he has to carry his enemy on his shoulders.

— *Panchtantra*

Where did the mighty
with all their splendour go?
All we have now is records of their passing show.

— *Hitopadeśa*

Never doubt a man with ambition
even though he trips while trying.
Though you may overturn a fire,
but a flame will never burn downwards.
— *Hitopadeśa*

For the ambitious,
a million miles don't appear too far.
Others are contented with what they have in hand.
— *Hitopadeśa*

For those who are contented with what they have,
fate has done all for them
and will do no more.
— *Hitopadeśa*

Just as the sun begins to set and it's time for the lotus flower to close, but the bee continues to explore the heart of the lotus, oblivious of the danger the ambitious scarcely reflect on the risk they run with their eye glued to their goal.
— *Panchtantra*

Afraid of foreign lands, crows, deer and cowards,
listless and without energy,
they stay and die in their own country.
— *Panchtantra*

Small minds get flustered with little efforts.
Resolute minds undertake big tasks
and pursue them with constancy.

— *Hitopadeśa*

Anger

If you must feel anger, then feel angry at anger itself.
— Chanakya

A forest heals and grows again,
even when cut down and burnt.
But harsh words never heal,
preventing new shoots from springing up.
— *Panchtantra*

A gambler plays continuously,
uninterrupted by nightfall,
or even by his mother's death.
And he loses his temper, when faced with difficulties.
— Chanakya

Change

If there was no birth, no death,
no old age, nor separation from those we love,
nor the transitory nature of all things,
how would there be any excitement in life?
— *Panchtantra*

Sulking lions locked up in cages;
Bruised elephants pricked on their head by their rider;
Listless cobras dulled into stupor by snake charmers;
Down and out scholars, dogged by anonymity;
Heroic warriors abandoned by their kings.
For Time, we are just an amusement,
to be swung back and forth like playthings.
— *Panchtantra*

Ailments are inevitable for humans,
misfortunes inevitable for the wealthy.
Parting of ways is built into a meeting,
all creation is so fleeting.
— *Hitopadeśa*

Everything we adore
beauty, youth, wealth, power and loved ones,
is as transitory as life itself.
— *Hitopadeśa*

As you rise from bed today,
what dangers lie in wait?
Illness, grief or your own death,
who knows what is your fate?

— *Hitopadeśa*

Everything in the realm of existence is in change
and is transitory.
Whatever comes, passes away,
whatever is born, must die.
Every living creature, like other things,
is a compound of elements;
sooner or later they must dissolve.

— From "The Parable of the Mustard Seed" in *Buddhist Parables*

The only universal law of the world,
and of God's worlds,
is that all things are impermanent.

— *Kisa Gotami* in conversation with the Buddha in *Buddhist Parables*

Union surely makes it clear,
that parting too will come to be.
Birth itself declares,
that death is an inevitability.

— *Hitopadeśa*

Just as river currents flow forward,
and never backwards,
days turn into nights, and so on,
till our lives fade away.

— *Hitopadeśa*

You can only enjoy riches and youth,
the friendship of the wicked, food
and women, but a short time.

— *Panchtantra*

Beauty, youth, wealth, power,
loved ones and life itself —
there is no doubt
that they are all transitory.

— *Hitopadeśa*

Where did all the mighty go
with their retinues of splendour?
All the earth bears now
is witness to their "passing show."

— *Hitopadeśa*

A body will have ailments
and misfortunes will reside in men's lives.
All meetings must result in parting
and all creation is fleeting.

— *Hitopadeśa*

We only notice the body's decay when it dies
though it wastes away throughout our lives.
— *Hitopadeśa*

Passing clouds, bad friends,
new grain, young women,
youth and riches —
Oh! How fleeting is their pleasure.
— *Panchtantra*

Meeting is a sure sign that parting will follow.
Birth makes it inevitable that death will follow.
— *Hitopadeśa*

From the day you come to stay in your mother's womb,
you begin a ceaseless journey that brings you near death
every day.
— *Hitopadeśa*

Character & Ethics

How you deal with people indicates your inner core.
That is the essence of behaviour.
— Chanakya

Men commit sinful acts
for the sake of this wretched body;
perishable, ungrateful and a bag of impurities.
— *Hitopadeśa*

A man achieves perfection
when he does not envy another's wealth,
looks at wives of other men without passion,
and sees a reflection of himself in all creatures.
— *Hitopadeśa*

Restrain anyone pursuing a wrong path even if it is your own family, a friend or the king. You may find yourself controlled by their will if you fail to correct their ways.
— *Panchtantra*

A man who has done something wrong,
enters the room with faltering steps,
a pale face, stuttering, stammering and trembling,
and eyes cast down.
— *Panchtantra*

Act with integrity and fairness,
irrespective of the state of life you are in.

— *Hitopadeśa*

A man with character speaks nicely even when wealthy, has humility even when brave, and is kind in spite of his strength.

— *Hitopadeśa*

Just like a storm bends tall trees, but not the grass,
the strong test their might with equals.

— *Hitopadeśa*

An angry man needs no reason to fly into a temper.
A saint finds no reason to lose his calm.
Sugar and lime hold their own taste.
Each one of us has a distinctive character.

— *Panchtantra*

Flowers have fragrance even after being plucked.
An elephant continues to have sex even when old.
Sugarcane remains sweet even when crushed.
Great men keep their good qualities
even when they are in misfortune.

— Chanakya

The unethical remain curled like a dog's tail,
no matter how much you try to straighten them.

— *Hitopadeśa*

What good is the finest fragrance, the purest pearl, or
the sweetest candy, if it requires you to compromise
your self respect and integrity.
— *Panchtantra*

A hungry dog will feed on bones and scrap;
a lion will hunt down an elephant
but not eat a fox in his grasp.
In a crisis,
every creature shows its true colours.
— *Hitopadeśa*

It is better to be silent than utter falsehoods.
It is better to beg than to prosper by stealing.
It is better to die than to put your faith in rogues.
— *Hitopadeśa*

Self-respect is lost in servitude.
Darkness is lost in moonlight.
All activity is lost in old age.
All virtue is lost in seeking favours.
— *Hitopadeśa*

Buying sex with money,
depending on others for a living,
tying the mind up with trivial pursuits;
men should avoid all three.
— *Hitopadeśa*

Fear danger as long as it is far away.
Stand and fight with courage when it's face to face.

— *Hitopadeśa*

Just like streams dry out in summers,
arrogant and unintelligent men produce no results.

— *Hitopadeśa*

The wise don't whine about their losses, or their family problems or their failures, or their mental anguish.

— *Hitopadeśa*

Virtue is the one feature that separates men from animals. Otherwise, in fear and hunger, sex and rest, there is nothing to differentiate the two.

— *Hitopadeśa*

The heaven's doors are open to those who stay away from violence, control their temptations and are ready to help everyone.

— *Hitopadeśa*

The only friend that will follow you to death and beyond is your character and virtue. All others will perish.

— *Hitopadeśa*

Rarely do you find men with these three qualities:

- humility in prosperity;
- calm in adversity; and
- steadiness in warfare.

— *Hitopadeśa*

How can a wise man do acts
that ruin his reputation, make him lose public trust
and send him down into a pit.

— *Panchtantra*

So long as a wrong deed does not bear fruit,
a man may mistake it for honey.
But when it ripens, he will suffer grief.

— *Sutta Pitaka*

It takes great effort to haul a heavy boulder up a hill; but only a moment to let it slip down. The same it is for men building a reputation.

— *Hitopadeśa*

Even if misdeeds result in a profit,
their final result cannot be good.
Honey laced with poison can only result in a fatality.

— *Hitopadeśa*

Man goes to great heights or sinks by his actions.
Like one who builds a tower
or the one who digs a mine.

— *Hitopadeśa*

A true and upright man speaks with calm, is cheerful, has a smiling face but a defiant eye. He speaks clearly, with a firm tone and a hint of pride.

— *Hitopadeśa*

Lust, anger, greed, infatuation, arrogance, envy. These six enemies have destroyed many rulers by bringing them under their control. Those with character must steer clear of these six enemies.

— Chanakya

It takes great effort to roll a rock up a hill.
All it takes is a simple tug to roll it back down.
Integrity works the same way.

— *Panchtantra*

Charity & Philanthropy

The rich man's wealth is only that
which he spends and gives away.
For when he is gone,
with the rest and his wives,
others will play.

— *Hitopadeśa*

What you give and what you live on
is your only wealth.
The rest you guard, for others to inherit.

— *Hitopadeśa*

Bees gather honey with great effort for others to enjoy.
So, too, a miser hordes his riches for others.

— *Panchtantra*

A man should use his money to provide for his necessities and to give to charity, but not to hoard, for the bees hoard their honey and people take it away.

— *Panchtantra*

You should always want to get something you don't have. And when you get it, guard it in a manner that it will continue to grow. And once it has grown, share it with those who need it.

— *Hitopadeśa*

The man who lets his wealth sit idle,
finds no happiness in this world or the next.
He is nothing but a fool performing a watchman's role.
— *Hitopadeśa*

Give not because it needs to be done,
or for the sake of any return.
— *Hitopadeśa*

Water drained out of a tank regularly
keeps foul smell away.
Money earned and used for charity
does the same.
— *Hitopadeśa*

Life is like the moon's fleeting reflection in water.
Those who understand this well,
must do as much good as possible.
— *Hitopadeśa*

The mere warmth of wealth is sufficient to enhance the spirit and energy of most men. Why not share this warmth by giving away some of it?
— *Panchtantra*

Counsel

A bad adviser destroys a ruler,
robbers ruin a city,
bad women ruin homes,
and bad sons destroy a family.
— Chanakya

Just as knowledge is wasted by lack of practice,
rulers are ruined by the faults of their retainers,
women are ruined by daily merriment,
and fields ruined by bad seed.
— Chanakya

Wise men don't serve rulers who listen to ministers
saying whatever pleases the ruler.
— Chanakya

A minister should be able to suggest war strategies,
take quick decisions in personal matters,
exhibit happiness in the achievements of a friend,
and show boldness in the affairs of the state.
— Chanakya

Like a pot, an adviser must yield little
and hold a lot.
— *Hitopadeśa*

It is easy to find men
who always speak what is pleasant to hear.
It is hard to find a man who is willing
to speak or listen to the truth.

— *Hitopadeśa*

Those who trust strangers and disregard the advice of their friends and trusted counsel, are heading for destruction.

— *Panchtantra*

When kings or elephants go berserk driven by their pride or arrogance, the blame falls on those who are guiding them.

— *Hitopadeśa*

A good minister must advise the king not to do things that suit his whim. It is better that the king be annoyed by such advice than be destroyed by doing what he should avoid.

— *Hitopadeśa*

The consequences of unpleasant but good advice are always positive as long as such advice is given by an unbiased giver and received by a willing acceptor. Wherever both are found, prosperity flourishes.

— *Hitopadeśa*

Give advice to those wise enough to appreciate it.
Birds gave advice to monkeys
only to be driven away by them.

— *Hitopadeśa*

For the wicked,
a hundred favours count as none.
For those without an ear for music,
a hundred verses of a poem are a waste.
For those who pay no heed,
pleading a hundred times is futile.
For the mindless, good counsel has no hold.

— *Hitopadeśa*

The adviser shall always be at the king's side, neither too close nor to far away, and:

- Not talk slyly against other advisers;
- Not say things which are not carefully thought out and which are untrue, uncultured, or outside his knowledge;
- Neither talk in secret with another [adviser] nor become quarrelsome in public debate;
- Not interrupt while another is speaking;
- Not antagonise the powerful; and
- Not associate with disreputable women, pimps, envoys of neighbouring kings, those supporting the enemy, dismissed officers, wicked people, those who form a group for a single objective nor with specialised guilds.

— *Arthaśāstra*

The adviser may even remain silent when asked for his opinion but shall never say anything that is unwelcome to, or likely to provoke, the king. Even competent people may be cast out if they say unwelcome things — and undesirable people who know the mind and inclinations of the monarch may become favourites.

— *Arthaśāstra*

A king should ascertain the views of his advisers indirectly. He should pose to them a problem similar to the one in mind and then ask for their advice with questions, like: "Supposing this, or that, were to happen, how should we proceed?" He can then follow their advice in the hypothetical case. By this method, one obtains advice while maintaining secrecy.

— *Arthaśāstra*

Advisers, when asked questions about hypothetical situations, either do not take seriously nor talk about them openly. In neither case is the purpose served. Therefore, the king should consult only those who will be involved in the task to be accomplished. Both objectives — getting sound advice and maintaining secrecy — will then be achieved.

— *Pisuna*

A wise ruler respects advisers who warn him of the dangers of transgressing the limits of good conduct, reminding him of the times prescribed for various duties, and caution him even when he errs in private.

— *Arthaśāstra*

Those who do not listen to good advice will face destruction.

— Chanakya

A king's mind is hard to figure out,
and 'tis hard to be a king's advisor.
Even if you mean well,
a king could turn hostile,
yet grant favours to those who cause him injury.

— *Hitopadeśa*

The power of a ruler remains uncontested if augmented by the counsel of good ministers.

— Chanakya

The fish's power lies in water,
and those of lions in their domain.
Of soldiers in their forts and towers,
and of kings in their adviser's hands.

— *Hitopadeśa*

Without far sighted advisers,
a king's fall is certain and not too distant.
— *Panchtantra*

Crisis / Adversity

Keep your calm even when you are caught in the eye of a storm and you will make it to safety. This quality will also help you enjoy happiness and more.

— *Panchtantra*

No sooner had I passed the storm and thought that I had crossed the ocean, another storm loomed ahead of me. Problems usually pile up together at our worst moments.

— *Panchtantra*

God himself cannot take away
what a man is destined to have.
What is mine cannot be another's,
and what's not mine, I don't grieve for.

— *Panchtantra*

Brooding in a crisis will only increase the pain.

— *Panchtantra*

Even small troubles become serious
for one already under attack.

— Chanakya

The mind weakens when a crisis draws near.

— *Hitopadeśa*

It takes a crisis for a man to realize the worth of his power, mind, servant, spouse and family.

— *Hitopadeśa*

Decision Making

Decisions based on pride and greed, anger or fear, are bound to be wrong.

— *Panchtantra*

A case in dispute is four-legged. It depends on what is right according to principles, evidence, custom, and the ruler's orders. The last one overrules all the others

— Chanakya

I don't know what I need to do now.
Just like the man who can't let go
or hold on to the snake he grabs
when drowning in a lake.

— *Hitopadeśa*

Impulsive decisions in a crisis lead to disaster.
Think your actions through
even in times of peril.

— *Hitopadeśa*

I don't count as true
words said by those who call others "fools."
They call each other so,
because they deem their own view "truth."

— The Buddha as quoted in *Sutta Nipata*

Only a fool thinks he did the right thing when his actions have not demonstrated results. But when the results are out, he suffers grief.

— *Sutta Pitaka*

Wisdom lies in making decisions in a crisis.
Disaster lies at every step if we vacillate.

— *Hitopadeśa*

Never can a single person arrive at the right decision. The work of government is dependent on knowledge — that which the king personally knows, that which is reported to him, and that which he has to infer. To find out what is not known, to clarify doubts when there are alternatives, to obtain more information when only a part is known — all these can be done only with the help of advisers. Hence, a king shall conduct his deliberations with advisers of mature intelligence. Despise no one, but listen to all views; for, a wise man pays heed to all sensible advice, even that of a child.

— *Arthaśāstra*

Be it counsel, heroic feat, swift attack or quick retreat, don't stay immersed in thought, when the time is ripe to act.

— *Hitopadeśa*

A prudent man must do what he must,
both noble or despicable, with an eye to the future.

— *Panchtantra*

Destiny

At a critical moment
of an attack in battle,
or a fire at home,
or stuck in a storm in the middle of an ocean,
what is not to be, will not be,
what is to be, will never be lost.
— *Panchtantra*

What is not to be can never be,
what will be, occurs effortlessly.
What is not destined is lost,
even as it lies in your palm.
— *Panchtantra*

Is it the right time?
Is it the right place?
Who are my friends?
What's the risk, and what the benefit?
And what am I?
What is my power and strength?
One should ponder over these questions
again and again.
— *Panchtantra*

If your luck is not with you,
even wealth that comes flies away,
taking with it something more as it goes.

— Panchtantra

Determination & Resolve

The greatness of successful men
lies in not giving up what they begin.
Even when hard times bring a swell of problems.
— *Panchtantra*

Just as young beautiful women
despise an old husband's touch,
fortune is repelled from men without determination.
— *Panchtantra*

Success may elude you even if try your best.
Don't blame yourself for failure, though,
as fate can muzzle even the most determined men.
— *Panchtantra*

Combine guts with strategy, put your plans to execution, support your action with enthusiasm, and fortune will find you.
— *Panchtantra*

Just as a potter uses clay to shape what he wishes,
a man will reap what he sows in life.
— *Hitopadeśa*

Never doubt a determined man's ability to bounce back
though he may appear down and out.
A flame will not burn downwards,
even when a candle is held upside down.

— *Hitopadeśa*

Steel your thoughts like a fortress and attack temptation with the weapon of knowledge and discipline; and don't rest even when you have conquered it.

— *Sutta Pitaka*

I have drunk foul smelling water
and have slept on clumps of grass.
I have endured the parting
of my loved ones with pain.
I have winced and spoken humbly
to strangers and have trudged on foot.
O Desire, is there anything else
you would make me do.

— *Panchtantra*

Discretion

You become dependent on as many men
as to whom you have told a secret.
— Chanakya

Those who cannot keep a secret,
make themselves vulnerable and will perish.
Just like a snake which lives on an anthill
and tells others about it.
— *Panchtantra*

The wise can gauge your intentions
from the change in your face's colour,
or your shifting eyes and body is stance,
and from the tone of your voice.
One should exchange advice in private.
— *Hitopadeśa*

If private consultations get shared by more than two people, they then become no better than public news. All confidential discussions should be held person to person.
— *Hitopadeśa*

There is no cure for evils which a leak from the counsels of the king will bring.
— *Hitopadeśa*

Age, monetary status and sexual relations, must be kept concealed with every care.

— *Hitopadeśa*

A man may tell some things to his wife, other to his close friends and some to his children. All of them deserve his trust. But he should not reveal all matters to any one person.

— *Hitopadeśa*

Just as a bridge can be overrun by the stream,
an unguarded secret will not remain a secret.
Intrigue can break a friendship,
and a coward will be exposed by his actions.

— *Hitopadeśa*

None must know what a king sets out to do.
Only those who have to implement it
should know when the work is begun,
or when it has been completed.

— *Arthaśāstra*

Let the wise man guard his thoughts,
for that makes them difficult to be perceived.
Thoughts well guarded bring happiness.

— *Sutta Pitaka*

Ego

An egotistical man's senses have scorn for others and a conviction that he is right and he ranks all his rivals as "sorry brainless fool."

— The Buddha as quoted in *Sutta Nipata*

With the theories he has devised, the stubborn wrangles on through life.

— The Buddha as quoted in *Sutta Nipata*

No dogmatist can win, by self concocted views.

— The Buddha as quoted in *Sutta Nipata*

Endeavour

Don't expect things to happen without hard work.
Oil cannot be extracted without pressing oil seeds.
— *Panchtantra*

Silk is spun by a worm.
Gold is found in rocks.
A lotus grows in mud.
The moon reflects in the ocean.
Fire flashes out of wood.
A person's shines from his efforts.
Of what consequence is his birth?
— *Hitopadeśa*

Water falls from the skies
but also gushes by digging deep into earth.
Fate may be powerful but effort is powerful too.
— *Panchtantra*

You must make an effort even if fortune is in your favour.
— *Hitopadeśa*

Just as no vehicle moves with only one wheel, luck won't move without endeavour.
— *Hitopadeśa*

Just as you cannot clap with a single hand,
deeds will not bear fruit without perseverance.
— *Panchtantra*

Perseverance, not wishes, get results.
Deer don't just walk into the mouths of lions.
— *Panchtantra*

Just as a lamp placed on a blind man's palm
does little to help him;
learning can do little to help those who shy away from strenuous effort.
— *Panchtantra*

Fortune is surely yours if you constantly strive.
Cock a snook at fate with all your strength;
only a coward wails his fate;
What's important is to have tried,
even if the effort fails.
— *Panchtantra*

When men are determined,
gods come through for them.
— *Panchtantra*

A lion relishes the meat of animals he hunts.
But if his favourite food does not come his way,
you will never catch him eating grass.
— *Hitopadeśa*

Throw a dog a bone with barely any meat on it and hardly enough to kill its hunger, yet he laps it up. But a lion throws aside the fox that lands right in its lap, to chase even the meanest elephant in the jungle.

— *Hitopadeśa*

You may not get anywhere
if you take the risks of enterprise.
But if you take the risk and survive,
success will surely be yours.

— *Hitopadeśa*

God bestows favours on zealous men,
and scorns the idle who depend entirely on luck.
Brush destiny aside, then,
and try with all your might.
If you still fail, find out what went wrong,
then try again.

— *Panchtantra*

Don't expect results without the risks of enterprise.
And if you take that risk and survive,
you will surely rise.

— *Hitopadeśa*

Warriors, scholars and beautiful young women
make a home for themselves wherever they go.

— *Panchtantra*

Come here, go there, sit, stand and stay,
be silent, speak, and even go.
A servant plays to an employer's every wish
gripped by the hope of a better life.

— *Hitopadeśa*

Just as even brilliant moonlight does not shine on a snow covered mountain, a man undertaking a task without knowledge of his resources and energies will see his best efforts fail.

— *Panchtantra*

Immense ends can be achieved by little means;
a rock can be lifted with a piece of wood.

— *Hitopadeśa*

Results cannot be won without painstaking effort;
just as fruit cannot grow instantly in an orchard.

— *Hitopadeśa*

Fortune comes to those who strive
even though their efforts may not always succeed.
It is sure that without effort,
there will never be success.

— *Hitopadeśa*

Akin to moonlight on the snow capped mountain, efforts undertaken without appropriate resources and energies will rarely shine.

— *Hitopadeśa*

Greed

The crane feasted on all kinds of fish.
Not sparing the big, the middling or even the small.
Till extreme greed did it in
and it died caught in a crab's claws.

— *Hitopadeśa*

Greed creates strong cravings
and affects one mentally.
It leads men to lasting misery.

— *Hitopadeśa*

Even the learned, the discerning and those who have no doubts or confusion, suffer when deluded by greed.

— *Hitopadeśa*

Greed breeds delusion, desire and chagrin, and that is sure to lead to destruction.

— *Hitopadeśa*

Greed clouds the minds of even the learned and the rich. It drives them to do horrendous deeds and roam strange, impassable regions.

— *Panchtantra*

One with a hundred, longs for a thousand.
One with a thousand, yearns for millions.
One who lords over millions,
wants to rule a kingdom.
The kings aim to gain Paradise itself.
— *Panchtantra*

The hair turns white or withers away with age
and teeth age and decay.
With age, the eyes see less
and the ears hear less.
One thing alone never ages — greed.
— *Panchtantra*

What will a man not do for money.
He will cast suspicion on the righteous
and praise the wicked.
— *Panchtantra*

Avarice, I bow to you.
You make men do things
they ought not have done
and wander in places
where they ought not have gone.
— *Panchtantra*

Just as it is impossible not to taste honey or poison that one may find at the tip of one's tongue, so it is impossible for one dealing with the royal treasury not to taste, at least a little bit, of the king's wealth.

— *Arthaśāstra*

Knowledge & Learning

Without learning, even princes
endowed with youth and power, cannot shine.
They are no more than scented flowers.

— *Hitopadeśa*

A well dressed fool may be considered distinguished even in a council hall. And this impression may stick as long as he does not open his mouth.

— *Hitopadeśa*

Just as a piece of glass may pass off as diamond when set in gold, a fool may grow wise in the company of the learned.

— *Hitopadeśa*

Those with a desire to learn
listen attentively,
grasp what is taught,
retain the knowledge in memory,
know the difference
between the important and the unimportant,
draw inferences and deliberate
and imbibe the truth.

— Chanakya

Study, my son!
Read. Memorize what you learn.
A king is revered in his country.
The learned are revered everywhere.
— Chanakya

A blind king is better than a king with no learning.
At least the blind king can see through spies.
— Chanakya

Humility should be learnt from noble princes,
good speech from scholars,
falsehood from gamblers,
and cunning from women.
— Chanakya

Eight type of people do not know others' sorrow;
the ruler, the prostitute, death, fire, thief, infant, beggar,
and the rogue.
— Chanakya

Learn this from the crow:
Have sex in secrecy.
Pursue action discreetly.
Complete work in time.
Remain unruffled and don't trust anyone.
— Chanakya

A true intellect will absorb scientific knowledge just as a sponge absorbs the water it comes in contact with.

— Chanakya

When learning results in integrity and wealth,
it is called knowledge.

— Chanakya

Learning gives access to high company
even to the lowly,
and then fortune flows
just as streams do and join the sea.

— *Hitopadeśa*

Learning teaches manners
and that brings gainful patronage.
Patronage builds wealth,
the key to happiness and virtue in this age.

— *Hitopadeśa*

Of all the things wise men say,
learning is beyond compare.
It is always prized and cannot decay,
nor be seized or forced away.

— *Hitopadeśa*

No one attains knowledge by mere research.
Knowledge is attained by action,
not by all the theories you may know.

— The Buddha as quoted in *Sutta Nipata*

Apart from Consciousness,
no diverse truths exist.
Mere sophistry declares this "true"
and that view "false."

— The Buddha as quoted in *Sutta Nipata*

The wise spend their spare time in learning.
The fools in vice, sleep or recrimination.

— *Hitopadeśa*

Blow off ignorance little by little and in small steps;
just as a silversmith blows off the metal's impurities.

— *Sutta Pitaka*

Continue your journey alone if you have not yet met someone who is your equal or your better. There is no companionship and nothing to learn from those who don't match up to you.

— *Sutta Pitaka*

A fool who knows he is foolish is indeed wise.
But a fool who thinks he is wise
is indeed a fool.

— *Sutta Pitaka*

Having studied every text on policy and grasped the meanings of the texts in their entirety, yet unable to use this knowledge in action, of what use is the time spent on such rigorous education.

— *Panchtantra*

What can learning do to a man without intelligence?
Did it ever make sense to show a mirror to a blind man?
— *Hitopadeśa*

Just as trees grow and flourish
by the banks of a river,
men without wit or learning can grow and flourish
by keeping wise and mature advisers.
— *Hitopadeśa*

Learning imparts discipline only to those who have the following mental faculties:

- obedience to a teacher,
- desire and ability to learn,
- capacity to retain what is learnt,
- understanding and reflecting on what is learnt, and
- ability to make inferences by deliberating on the knowledge acquired.

— *Arthaśāstra*

Knowledge that does not enable control over your passions is of little use, much as intelligence, peace or fame are of little use if all we do is to show them off.
— *Panchtantra*

Instruction and training can promote discipline only in a person capable of benefiting from them; people incapable of self-discipline do not benefit.
— *Arthaśāstra*

Leadership

A general who enjoys the respect of his soldiers, will be backed by them and is hard to beat in war.
— *Hitopadeśa*

A lion needs no emblems of royalty,
nor training in polity.
His sovereignty comes from superior strength.
He rules, crowned simply by the words,
O King! Hail! O King!
— *Panchtantra*

A lion needs no rite of consecration
nor sacred ablution to be crowned king
by the animals in the jungle.
— *Panchtantra*

Only fools stay in the service of kings
who humiliate their servants.
When fools dominate,
the wise will stay away.
A state abandoned by the wise
is ruled without policy.
— *Hitopadeśa*

Just as a tree does not withdraw its shade
from one who comes to chop it down,
one should show hospitality even to foes.

— Hitopadeśa

Great leaders prosper greatly
when they work for the people's good.
It is only in their people's ruin,
that they find their own.

— Hitopadeśa

Even a king of lofty lineage, descended of a long line of kings, in possession of immense wealth, cannot keep his retainers, if he does not know his own strengths and weaknesses.

— Hitopadeśa

Without a king to lead,
a kingdom's subjects sink.
Just like a ship without a captain
left at the mercy of the sea gods.

— Hitopadeśa

You don't have to be strong and powerful to get the job done if you know how to leverage the skills of other men. A stone cannot cut anything but it can sharpen a knife.

— Panchtantra

A king must attend to urgent matters urgently.
Such matters can get out of hand
if consideration and decision are delayed.
— Chanakya

People prosper or decline
with their leader's fortunes.
Just like the lotus that blooms and shrivels
with the rising and setting of the sun.
— *Hitopadeśa*

People crumble before a king who wields a cruel stick but are quick to criticize a king who rules with compassion.
— *Panchtantra*

Those who vacillate in making decisions and fail to give direction are despised by their team.
— *Hitopadeśa*

Ministers despise rulers who vacillate and ignore the tasks of the state.
— *Hitopadeśa*

The general must be protected at all times
and at all costs.
The army falls if the general is lost.
Remember, a wheel cannot turn if the hub gives way.
— *Panchtantra*

When a king treats all his subjects equally,
he will demoralize those who are the best
and those who sustain his kingdom.
— *Hitopadeśa*

Kings are like clouds that bring rains for their people.
But while people can live even if rains fail,
they will not survive if a kingdom loses power.
— *Hitopadeśa*

A king concerned about his own future and well-being must not trust even a loyal adviser if he does not respect protocol during the course of his duties.
— *Panchtantra*

The wind is a friend of the forest fire.
The same wind blows out a candle.
Who in the world honors the insignificant and weak?
— *Panchtantra*

A king's rule is of little use if he does not please his subjects fulfil his responsibilities and protect his subjects.
— *Panchtantra*

A king enjoys a long and glorious reign
if he has a passion for virtue
and an aversion for vice.
— *Panchtantra*

A general who is insecure
will have his men desert him in crises.
A coward guarantees his own destruction
by running away from war.
— *Hitopadeśa*

One who keeps his treasury flowing,
whose spies operate covertly and bring information,
whose counsel provides sincere advice,
and one who never speaks unpleasantly,
will rule the earth right to the sea.
— *Hitopadeśa*

The king's duties are five:
to punish the wicked,
to reward good citizens,
to grow the treasury by just means,
to be impartial in granting favours,
and to grow the state's image.
— Chanakya

The characteristics of a king are five:
he sacrifices wealth in favour of the needy,
he sticks to virtues,
he enjoys the company of friends and relatives,
he is eager to adopt new methods, and
he leads from the front in war.
— Chanakya

The king who acts like a skilled gardener
stays longer in power.
Like the gardener,
he rehabilitates the uprooted ones,
watches the blooming ones,
strengthens the weak ones,
bends down the tall ones,
weakens the aggressive ones,
separates the clustered ones,
trims the thorny ones, and
protects the ones who have come up by themselves.

— Chanakya

Rulers are like snakes.
Both are hooded,
covered with protection,
prone to pleasures, cruel and crooked.
But both are controllable by counsel.

— Chanakya

A ruler should be wise, friendly, sacrificing, transparent in his dealings, should keep distance from his subjects and remain stable in pain and pleasure.

— Chanakya

Warriors of merit are five hundred times bold.
They can rout a whole army
being resolute and united in their role.

— *Hitopadeśa*

Men's minds are not steady.

— Chanakya

A king should adopt the lifestyle, dress, language and customs of the people he rules. People don't trust a ruler whose behaviour is contrary to their own.

— Chanakya

A ruler with good qualities, adept at statecraft and endowed with loyal subjects always wins and enjoys the entire earth even when he rules a small region.

— Chanakya

Classmates and friends, though trustworthy, should not be appointed as ministers. Having known the king so closely, they will not respect him, nor hold him in reverence.

— Chanakya

Fear danger when it is likely,
but display true valour when it's present.
In times of crisis,
great men display courage all the way.

— *Hitopadeśa*

Always keep the seed of advice concealed till implementation. It will have no germination if it is revealed.

— *Hitopadeśa*

Forgiveness to friend or foe
may be a sign of excellence for monks.
But when practised by kings,
it is foolish and senseless.

— *Hitopadeśa*

A lion is never crowned as king by other animals.
His sovereignty is evident in the kingdoms he rules.

— *Hitopadeśa*

Courage in crises
and forgiveness in victory,
chivalry in war
and eloquence in assembly,
this is the true nature of men of real stature.

— *Hitopadeśa*

The great stand firm even when battered,
the ocean stays steady
even though its shores crumble,
but shallow minds change and veer
on the pettiest pretexts;
just as grass starts to tremble at the lightest breeze.

— *Panchtantra*

Just as solid rock is not shaken by the wind,
leaders don't waver with praise or blame.
— *Sutta Pitaka*

Trust is at the root of respect and success. That's how an elephant becomes the head of his herd, and though the lion has sovereignty over the jungle, deer don't wait upon him.
— *Panchtantra*

If you see a man who is intelligent, and who shows you
what is to be avoided
follow that wise man
as you would one who reveals hidden treasures.
— *Sutta Pitaka* (Buddhist scriptures)

Wild, fierce, cruel by nature and harsh and disagreeable in every word he speaks; what success do you expect having crowned such a man the king?
— *Panchtantra*

As you would a leaky boat at sea,
avoid a person without learning,
a priest without knowledge,
and a king who cannot defend.
— *Panchtantra*

People bloom when their kings shine
and wilt away when sovereigns decline.
'Tis like the lotus and the sun,
the flower blooms as morning comes
and wilts when the day is done.

— *Hitopadeśa*

In war, the king should lead from the front.
For when masters lead,
even dogs tread like lions.

— *Hitopadeśa*

Kind and harsh,
sometimes false, at other times true,
magnanimous and miserly,
free and lavish in spending,
demanding in work;
a king should always wear many faces.

— *Hitopadeśa*

A leader's mind and quality shine only in a crisis, just as a physician's skill becomes evident when a patient is dying. True skill and wisdom may not show when everything is going well.

— *Hitopadeśa*

If a just king is attacked, he will be backed by all. His people's love and his virtues will make him very hard to beat.

— *Hitopadeśa*

To exercise leadership over men, it is critical to understand the state of mind of those under you. An experienced leader leverages this knowledge to exercise influence over his people.

— Hitopadeśa

These be the five tenets for a king:

- a king shall develop his state, namely augment its resources and power in order to enable him to embark on a campaign of conquest;
- the enemy shall be eliminated;
- those who help are friends;
- a prudent course shall always be adopted;
- peace is to be preferred to war.

— Arthaśāstra

All state activities depend first on the Treasury. Therefore, a king shall devote his best attention to it.

— Arthaśāstra

In the happiness of his subjects
lies the king`s happiness;
in their welfare, his own.
He shall not consider as good
only that which pleases him
but treat as beneficial for himself
whatever pleases his subjects.

— Arthaśāstra

A king should be diligent in foreseeing the possibility of crises, try to avert them before they arise, overcome those which happen, remove all obstructions to economic activity and prevent loss of revenue to the state.

— *Arthaśāstra*

A wise ruler

- exercises self-control, having conquered the temptations of the senses,
- cultivates the intellect by association with intellectuals,
- keeps his eyes open through spies,
- promotes the security and welfare of the people,
- ensures the observance of rules by authority and example,
- improves his own discipline by continuing his learning in all branches of knowledge, and
- endears himself to his people by enriching them and doing good to them.

— *Arthaśāstra*

A ruler should collect revenues by sustaining the source of revenue, much as milk comes from nurturing the cow not selling it.

— Chanakya

Impoverishment, greed and disaffection are engendered among the subjects when the king:

- Does what ought not to be done and fails to do what ought to be done;
- Fails to give what ought to be given and exacts what he can not rightly take;
- Does not punish those who ought to be punished but punishes those who do not deserve to be;
- Arrests those who should not be arrested but fails to arrest those who should be seized;
- Indulges in wasteful expenditure and destroys profitable undertakings;
- Does not carry out his part of what had been agreed upon.

— *Arthaśāstra*

The king shall be ever active in the management of the economy. The root of wealth is economic activity and lack of it brings material distress. In the absence of fruitful economic activity, both current prosperity and future growth will be destroyed. A king can achieve the desired objectives and abundance of riches by undertaking productive economic activity.

— *Arthaśāstra*

A king with a depleted treasury eats into the very vitality of the citizens and the country.

— *Arthaśāstra*

A king shall employ, without hesitation, the methods of secret punishment against traitors in his own camp and against enemies; but he should do so with forbearance, keeping in mind the future consequences as well as immediate results.

— *Arthaśāstra*

Inaccessible rulers destroy the people.

— Chanakya

The king of the jungle — the lion
dwells in the woods,
alone and without emblems of royalty.
Unlearned, untrained in polity,
his superior strength gives him sovereignty.
He rules, crowned simply by the words,
O King! Hail! O King!

— *Hitopadeśa*

Rulers swayed by anger are killed by mob fury. Rulers addicted to pleasures are destroyed by enemies and diseases caused by decadence and vice.

— Chanakya

Leaders need learn three things from a donkey:
Don't give up even when tired.
Find comfort in heat and cold.
And always be satisfied.

— Chanakya

An arrow may or may not kill a person
but words from a popular leader can destroy a king.
— Chanakya

A ruler should collect revenues without destroying the source much as a gardener plucks flowers without destroying the roots.
— Chanakya

One who keeps his treasury in order,
whose spies covertly carry out their trade,
whose deals are made in secret,
who never speaks unpleasantly,
he will rule the earth right to the sea.
— *Hitopadeśa* (Adaptation)

Management / Governance

While his personal knowledge and the reports coming to him give the king an idea of the accomplishment of his government, he has to infer for himself what his officials have failed to do.

— *Arthaśāstra*

Wise men make use of even a child's word.
Don't we use a candle when there is no sunlight?

— *Hitopadeśa*

Excesses expenditure,
lack of proper inspection,
laxity in collecting revenues,
and exercising remote authority,
all are evils in governing.

— *Hitopadeśa*

An employee must speak out even when his view has not been solicited. When there are wrong decisions, or the situation is grave or critical, or when time is passing by and something needs to be done.

— *Hitopadeśa*

Employees can be rated as superior, mediocre and bad. They should be assigned jobs according to their ratings.

— Chanakya

Don't trust those who don't trust others.
In fact, don't trust even those
who are far too trustworthy.
— Chanakya

Employees who are satisfied,
have honest aspirations,
are vigilant, not lazy
and stable in happiness and sorrow
are rare in this world.
— Chanakya

A person who the ruler trusts over long periods of time is likely to take over everything from the ruler and pose as a ruler himself.
— Chanakya

Wise men hide their secrets and feelings by expressing and gesticulating the opposite of how they are feeling. They show love when they feel hatred, pleasure when they are sad and determination when they are afraid.
— Chanakya

No gift of land, money or gold,
nor that of food and shelter;
Of all the gifts you can give to your team,
is the best the gift of security.
— *Hitopadeśa*

The army must be kept under several commands.
That will ensure that the entire army will not cross over
to the enemy.

— Chanakya

When physicians and ministers
tell kings only what is pleasant,
The rulers will surely lose
their health, virtue and treasury in due course.

— *Hitopadeśa*

Arbitrary power cannot coexist with the rule of law.
Light and darkness cannot be found in the same place.

— *Hitopadeśa*

It is better to have
a small force of men of quality
rather than a grand line up of many.
If the weak crack in battle,
the strong will break with them.

— *Hitopadeśa*

Give the job to a man who has the competence for it.
Even the intelligent will mess up
when they lack experience.

— *Hitopadeśa*

Do not argue
even if you have to give way a hundred times.
To argue without a cause is a fool's pursuit.
— Hitopadeśa

Just as light makes owls go blind, good advice to a man whose mind is clouded with conceit, will only inflame and madden him.
— Panchtantra

All harsh talk is not poison,
so look in it for what can benefit you.
Not all sweet talk is honey,
so beware of treachery.
— Panchtantra

A forest can heal and grow again
even though it has been cut down and burnt.
But you can never heal the damage
caused by harsh words.
— Panchtantra

To be effective, a man's speech must be wise
and come out of deep reflection.
It must be measured and used to improve things.
— Panchtantra

Don't trust those unworthy of trust
and don't trust those whom you trust.
Such trust may put you in such perils
as could destroy you completely.
— *Panchtantra*

The following are the characteristics of a good edict:

- Topical order stating the principal subject first and arranging the rest logically.
- Non-contradiction in ensuring that the order is not incompatible with one made earlier, throughout the edict.
- Completeness in avoiding redundancy or deficiency of letters, words and subject matter; citing reasons, quotations and illustrative examples; avoidance of tired words (i.e. cliches); and using appropriately expressive words.
- Sweetness in using words which are pleasant and precise in their meaning.
- Dignity by avoiding vulgarism.
- Lucidity by using words which are well-known

— *Arthaśāstra*

Just as one plucks fruits from a garden as they ripen, so shall a king have the revenue collected as it becomes due. Just as one does not collect unripe fruits, the king shall avoid taking wealth that is not due because that will make the people angry and ruin the very sources of revenue.

— *Arthaśāstra*

When a king treats all his advisers alike, without regard to their contribution, he will lose those who sustain him and his power will wane over time.

— *Hitopadeśa*

In order to make the discontented happy, conciliation shall be the method used. If conciliation fails and they continue to be unhappy, they shall be used to collect taxes and fines so that they may incur the wrath of the public. When the people come to hate them, they shall be eliminated either by inciting a popular revolt against them, or by secret punishment.

— *Arthaśāstra*

The following are defects to be avoided in a ruler's edict:

- Absence of charm by using bad paper and writing unattractively, unevenly and illegibly resulting in clumsiness.
- Contradiction in making part of the edict incompatible with another part.
- Repetition.
- Bad grammar in using wrong gender, number, tense or case.
- Confusion when mistakes of arrangement are made; Examples are; dividing into paragraphs where inappropriate or not marking new paragraphs where they should be.

— *Arthaśāstra*

A king can reign only with the help of others; one wheel alone does not move a cart. A king should therefore appoint advisers and listen to their advice.

— *Arthaśāstra*

Fear, lack of employment and resentment are the only reasons why a vassal or ally leaves the king.

— *Arthaśāstra*

The king must refuse to renegotiate with one who left and returns for no reason, and one who has harmed the king.

— *Arthaśāstra*

Deliberations must not be unduly delayed once an opportunity for action arises.
No one who belongs to the side likely to be adversely affected by the project shall be consulted.

— *Arthaśāstra*

Managing Human Resources

Intelligence, perseverance and dexterity shall be evaluated by examining a candidate's past performance, while eloquence, boldness and presence of mind shall be ascertained by interviewing him personally. Watching how he deals with others will show his energy, endurance, ability to suffer adversities, integrity, loyalty and friendliness. From his intimate friends, the king shall find out about his strength, health and character, whether he be lazy or energetic, fickle and steady. The candidate's amiability and love of mankind shall be ascertained by personal observation.

— *Arthaśāstra*

If a king slights someone he has honoured earlier, he will at all times work towards his downfall.

— *Hitopadeśa*

Speak in private if you wish to say something which is unpleasant even if it is for the listener's good.

— Chanakya

Make sure the rewards are commensurate with the task you expect people to perform.

— Chanakya

You should leave your employer under the following circumstances:

- Your work gets destroyed before completion;
- Your powers are reduced;
- Your work is treated like a commodity;
- Your hopes are frustrated;
- You are eager to consider new ventures;
- You lose the confidence of your boss;
- You are in conflict with powerful people.

— Chanakya

Those who serve rulers are playing with fire and must always make sure they are protected or have an exit option.

— Chanakya

A ruler is hated if he metes out heavy punishment and despised if he punishes lightly. Only a ruler who metes out punishment that is commensurate with the offence is respected.

— Chanakya

Just as gold is tested in four ways, by scratching, breaking, heating and breaking, there are four ways to check a man; his family, conduct, integrity and actions.

— Chanakya

You can only train those who fit the job. It is fruitless to train those who don't.

— Chanakya

To find persons of a particular type, you need people of the same type. Thus, you need a crook to catch a crook.

— Chanakya

Kings who don't punish the guilty and punish the innocent cause discontent among subjects.

— Chanakya

Employees should not be condemned on someone's accusation, but rewarded or punished after one's own investigation.

— *Hitopadeśa*

There is no greater fault or disruptive action than praising new people and admonishing the old.

— *Hitopadeśa*

'Tis best to remove wheat that is infected, a tooth that shakes, and an employee who is not motivated.

— *Hitopadeśa*

An employee long in service turns brazen even though he may be wrong. He holds his superior in disdain, as if his actions cannot be restrained.

— *Hitopadeśa*

The king should keep a constant supervision over officers responsible for money. You cannot get much water from a towel by wringing it once.

— *Hitopadeśa*

Not collecting what is due,
embezzling revenue,
lethargy, disinterest
and no care of what is best
are faults of a corrupt officer.
— *Hitopadeśa*

Just as plants need to be watered
before they bear fruit,
people need to be nurtured for them to perform.
— *Panchtantra*

Stupid if he stays silent, aggressive if he speaks,
lack of initiative if he is patient,
called impatient if he reaches out.
Even gods can't make clear
what an employee needs to do.
— *Hitopadeśa*

Some men will accept employment
for five silver pieces.
Others for a thousand.
Some can't be employed for any sum.
— *Hitopadeśa*

A king who wishes to lead,
should nurture his people
with gifts, honour and esteem,
just as a gardener waters his plants.
— *Panchtantra*

The lazy ruin their reputation,
the ill natured their teammates.
Those prone to vice, lose learning
and the miserly lose happiness.
Kings with irresponsible deputies
lose their sovereignty.

— *Hitopadeśa*

Seek those with integrity and enterprise.
Keep under watch rogues with enterprise.
Pity those with integrity but no enterprise;
and shun rogues with no enterprise.

— *Panchtantra*

A retainer from the enemy's camp,
or a deserter anxious to join your side is a villain,
false and untrustworthy,
untrue to his own nature and his team.

— *Panchtantra*

If he makes them equal to those not their equals,
if he honours them less than he does their equals,
if he appoints them to positions below their ability,
his officers will leave the king in all three cases.

— *Hitopadeśa*

Once employees see their leaders treat all alike, with no distinctions for the good and the bad, the zeal of the diligent and skilled among them wanes.

— *Hitopadeśa*

In a place where no difference is perceived between a priceless gem with an eye of fire and a fragment of pale crystal, how can trade flourish?

— *Hitopadeśa*

When a king smiles at you from far,
and takes care in asking how you are,
speaks cheerfully,
does not let your faults cloud his behaviour
and in your absence talks about your merits,
it is a clear sign
that he is favourably inclined towards you.

— *Hitopadeśa*

When a king deprives a courtier of wealth and honour, it is better he resign. Else, he may recognise his own defects and, in the light of his understanding of the king, reform himself.

— *Arthaśāstra*

O King, there are three types of men:
The best, the worst and those at par.
They should be appointed to tasks
that fit their description.

— *Hitopadeśa*

Your managers should swell your treasure
and not lie for even a single dime.

— *Hitopadeśa*

Employees, like jewellery,
should be kept in their designated place.
Diamonds cannot be put on ankles
and anklets cannot grace a forehead.

— *Hitopadeśa*

When diamonds are set on lead and not on gold,
they don't lose their glitter
but the setter is called a fool.

— *Hitopadeśa*

Never employ (give shelter) one whose character or family ties you cannot determine.

— *Hitopadeśa*

Priests, warriors and family should never be considered for managing the treasury.

— *Hitopadeśa*

Negotiating

It is possible to please someone
who has a specific reason for being angry.
But how can one find a way to please those
who hold a grudge without reason?
— *Hitopadeśa*

Good advisers resort to conciliation
and exercise calm and diplomacy in a difficult situation.
Those who choose an aggressive posture,
or an impolite course of action,
risk the fortunes of kings.
— *Panchtantra*

Lasting peace can be achieved
through friendship, mutual obligations, gifts and
marriage.
— *Hitopadeśa*

The only real peace is won through the giving of gifts.
— *Hitopadeśa*

A stronger enemy will only withdraw
if it gets something in return.
The way to peace can be found in giving gifts.
— *Hitopadeśa*

Conciliation is the key to build lasting success.
— *Hitopadeśa*

When a man knows that he has no obvious advantage over an equal, he should pursue a peaceful settlement. If he lets pride blind him, even an equal will destroy him — just like a clay pot hitting another clay pot will split into pieces.
— *Panchtantra*

A king should make peace with the enemy when he and the enemy both achieve equal progress in equal time, and both decline equally in equal time, and there is no change in their respective situations during the same period of time.
— Chanakya in *The Arthaśāstra*

No one does favours out of kindness or love.
The motivation usually lies in greed or fear
— or some need.
— *Panchtantra*

Seeing the enemy ready to grab everything,
a wise ruler tries to buy time by offering him a little.
Just as the ocean pacifies the fire
by offering it a small quantity of water.
— *Panchtantra*

Conciliation is always a better option to war.
Why take bitter medicine when honey can cure an illness?

— *Panchtantra*

Even if weapons are drawn and the kingdom is littered with losses, and the enemy's emissary speaks rudely, a king should not take his life.

— *Panchtantra*

A messenger knits together or breaks what is well knit;
so, too, a messenger does what is needed
to make enemies come to terms.

— *Panchtantra*

The object of an emissary is to fit words to facts of the issue and communicate in words as best as he can to bring about the desired results.

— *Panchtantra*

To negotiate, send a respected emissary.
Negotiations are bound to succeed in the hands of one who knows the right time and place of action.

— *Panchtantra*

To make peace, do not offer to one enemy
that which is likely to be taken anyway,
by force by another foe.

— Chanakya

Conciliation, bribes and intrigues are all doors open for the intelligent.

— *Panchtantra*

There are six kinds of conciliation:

- Praising merits: Appreciating the merits of the person's pedigree, personal qualities, occupation, good nature, learning or wealth, either personally or to third parties;
- Mutual connections: Extolling common relationships, such as blood relationship, relationship by marriage, a common teacher, a common ritual system, common friends or family connections;
- Mutual benefits: Explaining the advantages that will accrue to each of the two parties;
- Inducement: Raising the hopes by pointing out the beneficial results that will accrue to both, if a particular course of action is adopted;
- Identity of interest: Shown by placing oneself at the other's disposal;
- Awards and honours: Giving a high rank or awarding an honour.

— *Arthaśāstra*

A state whose resources have been depleted becomes a liability if acquired.

— Chanakya

The weaker king must offer, by one means or another, that which the other will, in any case, take by force. It is life that is worth preserving, not wealth which, being impermanent, can be given up without regrets.

— *Arthaśāstra*

Conciliation means protecting the people living in the villages and forests, protecting cattle herds and trade routes, handing back to the subjugated king those who displeased him, ran away from him, or did him harm.

— *Arthaśāstra*

A king may demand immediate payment of the amount as agreed upon or even more, if he wants to break a treaty, or wants to weaken his enemy by utilizing an opportunity to harass the enemy's people, or break up an alliance between the enemy and his friend, or apprehends an attack by the enemy.

— *Arthaśāstra*

A king, whose offer of peace is rejected by an equally powerful king, shall harass the other to the same extent that he is harassed.
Just as unheated pieces of iron cannot be welded together, there can be no union without heat.

— *Arthaśāstra*

A vassal or ally may violate a treaty for any of the following reasons:

- Seeing the results of his efforts on behalf of the king destroyed;
- Loss of power;
- Desire to sell his knowledge to a higher bidder;
- Feeling of hopelessness;
- Lack of trust in the king; or
- Conflict with a powerful person.

— *Arthaśāstra*

On Women

A man will remain his own master as long as he is not controlled by the sharp words of a woman.

— *Panchtantra*

A man believes a wrong to be a right and a hard way to be an easy way to do things when driven by the words of a woman.

— *Panchtantra*

Lions with flowing manes and fierce jaws,
elephants with gleaming tusks,
men of great intellect and battle heroes,
all turn weak-kneed in a woman's presence.

— *Panchtantra*

Women have four times more intelligence than men.
They are also six times more enterprising.
And their passion is eight times greater than men.

— *Hitopadeśa*

Whoever makes a place his home, guards it well.
But women live in our hearts and burn it unrelentingly.

— *Hitopadeśa*

All the world's knowledge cannot beat a woman's wit.
How then do we protect ourselves from women?
— *Panchtantra*

He is eternally in her trance
and always at her the beck and call
a woman he loves.
— *Hitopadeśa*

Women, as the gods well know,
have always been very fickle.
The men who guard them seem rather happy with that.
— *Hitopadeśa*

Women are like oil filled jars
and men like burning wicks.
You never keep fuel and fire together.
— *Hitopadeśa*

Women are always hard to please.
Neither gifts nor praise nor honest pleas
nor being helpful, strong or smart
is enough to win a woman's heart.
— *Hitopadeśa*

Nothing in this world is as sweet or bitter
as a beautiful woman.
We live by her presence
and die from her absence.
— *Panchtantra*

What will a man not do or grant
when a woman asks him.
— *Panchtantra*

What is in their heart
may not make it to their tongue.
What is on their tongue, finds no expression.
What they express, they don't act upon.
How strange are the ways of women.
— *Panchtantra*

There is no book of knowledge
that is superior to a woman's wit.
— *Hitopadeśa*

Never fall prey to a smart woman's charms
and never wish a woman's power to grow.
Let a man dote on her, and she will play with him
like he was her pet bird with clipped wings.
— *Hitopadeśa*

The lion may be the king of the jungle,
the elephants may have imposing tusks,
men may have great intellect and
heroes may have won battles
but all turn pale in a female's presence.
— *Hitopadeśa*

Planning & Preparedness

Let actions prove the efficacy of your plans.
Plans are meant to be acted upon,
not merely spoken about.

— Chanakya

Plans based on knowledge and experience,
and executed by shrewd advisers
will never fail.

— *Panchtantra*

Embarking on a venture on impulse,
with no thought to the strengths and weaknesses
of self or the enemy is simply asking for trouble.

— *Panchtantra*

Think with clarity and plan for contingencies.
And you will live happily.

— *Hitopadeśa*

What will be, will be.
What will not be, will never be.
When this is the remedy for all things,
why not just drink and not worry anymore?

— *Hitopadeśa*

Difficult situations bring grief and fear to an unprepared fool. They have no effect on those who plan ahead.

— *Hitopadeśa*

You are asking for trouble if you embark on any venture on impulse, with no review of your own or your competitor's strengths and weaknesses.

— *Panchtantra*

Action backed by deliberation, examination and consultation will fail under no circumstances.

— *Panchtantra*

Those who prepare for eventualities that can happen, celebrate.
Those who are caught napping, drown in sorrow.

— *Hitopadeśa*

Going to war without planning
is like a bird trying to fly at night.
One who goes to war fully prepared
is like an owl flying at night.

— *Hitopadeśa*

To rush headlong in impatience against a foe before knowing one's own strength and power is to court disaster, much like a moth that plunges into a fire.

— *Panchtantra*

Just as you cannot clap with one hand,
no plan can succeed without effort.
— Panchtantra

An enterprising man with skill and expertise is always a master of wealth. But the biggest failing of the most enterprising men is unplanned enterprise.
— Panchtantra

The five aspects of deliberating on any questions are:
- the objectives to be achieved;
- the means of carrying out the task;
- the availability of men and materials;
- deciding on the time and place [of action]; and
- contingency plans against failure.

— Arthaśāstra

Power

Wise men leverage their relationship with the rulers to help friends and destroy enemies.

— Chanakya

The tell—tale signs of a person in decline are:
weakness of hands, flashes of anger,
a waning facial glow and loss of power.
A setting sun also demonstrates the same signs.

— *Panchtantra*

Power alters the mind.

— Chanakya

A king is at fault if he gives too much power to a minister. By doing this, the goddess of sovereignty rests on both the king and minister. Such a burden is too much for her to bear and she is sure to abandon one in due course.

— *Hitopadeśa*

When a man loses power or wealth,
self esteem, pride, judgement and learning,
wit, social graces and understanding,
all seem to vanish.

— *Panchtantra*

Power is the basis of all treaties.
Only molten metal joins with another molten metal.

— Chanakya

Men are respected only for their positions.

— Chanakya

Purpose

A king who faces his enemies with courage
and will not yield does not need to fear defeat.
— *Hitopadeśa*

No one can tread the path for you,
neither God nor man.
You must tread it for yourself.
So begin now.
Be alert, and steadfastly alert.
Make the most sustained effort
of which you are capable.
Let nothing entice you to dally by the wayside,
neither self-indulgence,
nor the mistaken urge to self-punishment,
nor vain curiosity,
nor the desire for companionship.
Face uncompromisingly toward the goal
and victory will be won.
— *Sutta Pitaka*

There are no chances of reaching our goal if we don't have a sense of time and place, or of what is right and proper; or if we act without due deliberation.
— *Panchtantra*

Long is the night for him who is awake.
Long is the mile for him who is tired.
Long is life for him
who does not know his goal.
— Sutta Pitaka

As a calf can find its mother
amongst a thousand cows;
so does destiny select its performers
from amongst the multitude.
— Panchtantra

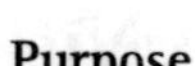

Risk

The wise protect themselves from both
— their own people and outsiders.
— Chanakya

Undetected disease is poison.
Women with drifting hearts are poison.
So is indulging in pleasure for a ruler.
— Chanakya

Just as it is not possible to know when fish drink water, so too it is difficult to find out when officers employed in the execution of works misappropriate money.
— Chanakya

You can fathom the flight path of birds but not the ways of those who hide their intentions.
— Chanakya

Just as bees pass by fresh blue lotuses
and blooming jasmine buds
to sit on elephant temples,
we pass on what is effortlessly ours
to seek delight in what is off limits.
— *Panchtantra*

Who does not lose money on bad advice?
Who does not fall ill with unhygienic food?
Who doe not become arrogant with wealth?
Who does not disappear with death?
Who can escape the torment
caused by a woman's words?

— *Hitopadeśa*

A wicked wife,
an untrustworthy friend,
and a snake inside one's home
all are sure to lead to a fatal end.

— *Hitopadeśa*

You can sleep easy in a home
where there are no snakes,
or where snakes have been seen but caught.
But when a snake is seen and is not caught,
you can only expect uneasy sleep.

— *Panchtantra*

Just as living with a snake is living in constant fear, one who has come over from the enemy is always a danger, because of his long association with the foe. Just as parasites take root and eventually smother a plant, one who has come from the enemy must always be feared as posing a danger even in the future.

— *Arthaśāstra*

Rivalry & the Art of Warfare

Don't take pleasure from an enemy's pain.
At the end of the day,
decay, old age, then death
is the final state for all.
— *Panchtantra*

To destroy those who made you suffer,
steel your heart and make it hard and ruthless,
and brush aside indecision and doubt
— but keep your speech as sweet as sugar.
— *Panchtantra*

Use conciliation, concession, dissension or invasion to destroy an enemy. An enemy should be destroyed by all means at hand.
— Chanakya

An enemy should be eliminated by taking the help of his enemy. A thorn can be extracted only by using another thorn.
— Chanakya

An enemy should be engaged in difficulties;
a daughter in a good family;
an able son in education
and a friend in integrity.

— Chanakya

Just like the collision of two clay pots,
a fight between equals destroys both.

— Chanakya

You cannot fight an enemy
who fights with no desire to live.

— Chanakya

Don't fight a powerful foe if you don't have to.
A cloud does not move ahead
if the winds in the opposite direction are strong.

— *Panchtantra*

Don't try to make peace or go to war if you are faced with a powerful and vicious enemy. Nothing except withdrawal works when your enemy has no restraint.

— *Panchtantra*

Make a call on the course of action
and then either retreat if you fear for your life,
or march forward thirsty for victory.

— *Panchtantra*

Under the present circumstances,
let's withdraw, O King!
It is not possible to go to war
or sue for peace
with a foe who is both strong and evil.
— *Panchtantra*

To convince a foe in such a way
that he leaves the field for you,
keep the conversation sweet but a resolve of steel.
— *Panchtantra*

All policy is, in essence,
one's own rise and the other's fall.
These are the only two ends to which wise men agree.
— *Hitopadeśa*

Only fools face an enemy without due thought,
thus making sure that they get his sword's embrace
— *Hitopadeśa*

Going to war with those stronger than oneself
is not ordained.
For if men will fight elephants,
they will surely perish.
— *Hitopadeśa*

Stay contracted and take some blows like a tortoise
but when the time comes, rise like a snake and strike
fiercely.

— *Hitopadeśa*

One archer on a wall
fights back a hundred sent to attack.
A hundred on a battlement can match a thousand.
That's why one must prepare
fortifications ahead of battle.

— *Hitopadeśa*

The fox on slippery muddy ground
can bring an elephant down.
What you cannot do by force,
you can achieve by choosing the right battleground.

— *Hitopadeśa*

With enemies there can be no peace,
no matter how good the pact.
You can heat water much as you please,
it will still put out a fire.

— *Hitopadeśa*

In blind arrogance,
men often insult a weak foe.
Only to see the foe growing unbeatable,
like an rampant disease.

— *Panchtantra*

Without first gaining the trust of their enemies,
even gods cannot win against them.
— *Panchtantra*

The wise root out one fiery foe
by means of another more fiery,
just as the pain from a thorn seems less
when pierced by an ever sharper thorn.
— *Panchtantra*

Whoever makes friends
with a foe far more powerful than himself,
is certain to be feeding himself poison.
— *Panchtantra*

There are points of vulnerability in a fort
if it is small or insecure,
or lacks the will to endure,
or is manned by timid soldiers,
with fools or scoundrels in command.
— *Hitopadeśa*

There are three methods to take a fort in war:
- a secret deal,
- a long blockage, or
- great courage.

— *Hitopadeśa*

When your partner becomes your competitor, he knows all your secrets — including your strengths and weaknesses. He can burn you like the fire that sparks inside a withered tree.

— *Hitopadeśa*

The too — forgiving lose ability to safeguard
even what they hold,
and then that could be grain or gold.

— *Hitopadeśa*

When it is futile to withdraw or hide,
go all out in war with all your might.

— *Hitopadeśa*

One thought that one should never avoid,
is that in a war both parties may get destroyed.

— *Hitopadeśa*

One should look for peace, even with those of one's size. You can never be sure of victory, if things finally end up in war.

— *Hitopadeśa*

Steel your heart till it becomes hard and ruthless.
Let your tongue be sweet as sugar.
Be decisive and have no doubts,
and finish the competition
at whose hands you have suffered before.

— *Panchtantra*

As flowing streams crack and split mountains,
in spite of the close — knit rocks.
So too well devised dissensions will not fail,
to undermine even the most formidable foe.
— *Panchtantra*

Only a fool will stake himself, his rule, his allies,
arms and reputation on the disturbance in balance,
uncertainty and destruction that a war brings.
— *Hitopadeśa*

Peace with foes of the same strength is wise.
Victory is never assured in such a war.
— *Hitopadeśa*

If you are cornered and have nothing to lose,
it's time to go to war.
— *Hitopadeśa*

The mightiest will be brought down if they fail to
destroy competition the instant it rears its head.
Problems and competition have a tendency to grow in
strength and magnitude if not nipped in the bud.
— *Panchtantra*

Taking an adversarial stance without understanding an
enemy's strength, we run the risk of defeat.
— *Panchtantra*

In circumstances where there are no gains to be made or defeat is imminent, a ruler avoids provocations that may lead to war.

— *Panchtantra*

An elephant with broken tusks beats a hasty retreat.
A weak ruler does the same
if he goes up against a strong foe.

— *Panchtantra*

It is easy to vanquish an enemy who is greedy, careless, unstable, timid, untrue, lazy and does not respect his soldiers.

— *Hitopadeśa*

Try peaceful solutions first;
a fight should be your last resort.
Even mighty warriors cannot guarantee victory in a battle.

— *Panchtantra*

Fodder, fuel, food and weapons should always be stocked up in the fortress in anticipation of an enemy's attack.

— Chanakya

Maintain peace with an enemy
till you figure out his weakness.

— Chanakya

Strike an enemy at his weakest point.

— Chanakya

Don't reveal your weakness.

— Chanakya

The residues of a defeated enemy may become active, just as disease, fire and debt can. Exterminate them completely.

— Chanakya

Don't ignore an enemy even if he appears weak. He may become dangerous in due course. After all, you need just a spark to light a fire in a haystack.

— Chanakya

Wise rulers don't ignore even the children of a surrendered enemy. They could prove dangerous in due course just as wild fires can break out even from dry leaves.

— Chanakya

Make peace with the enemy so long as times are bad. Attack when the right time comes.

— Chanakya

The enemy should not know your intentions.
One should hide one's intentions,
just as the tortoise withdraws its limbs
and watches the enemy's posture.

— Chanakya

A ruler must hide his weakness and magnify those of the enemy. His behaviour must replicate that of a moneylender's.

— Chanakya

A ruler in trouble should form alliances with all available.

— Chanakya

Finish a foe when he is down and out.
If you allow him to gather strength again,
he may become invincible.

— *Panchtantra*

If prosperity is what you want, don't rear up like a snake when a stronger enemy challenges you. It is best to bend like a twig by a stream in such circumstances.

— *Panchtantra*

Wise men retreat into their shells like a tortoise does and take the blows that come. When the time is ripe, they rear up like a snake ready to strike a deadly blow.

— *Panchtantra*

When it is clear that an enemy cannot be contained by conciliation, get ready for war. For, when fever cannot be controlled by cold packs, it needs be sweated out.

— *Panchtantra*

All times are favourable for a surprise attack on an enemy who has chinks in his armour and is vulnerable.

— *Panchtantra*

A ram draws back only to butt more fiercely.
A tiger crouches in fury before he attacks.
Hiding enmity deep in your heart,
and keeping your moves a secret,
wait, biding for the right time to attack
and endure everything till that right moment.

— *Panchtantra*

Harbour deep distrust and adopt a policy of duplicity when dealing with a powerful ememy. Offer peace and then go to war as the situation demands.

— *Panchtantra*

The choice of battlefield is critical.
A dog can drag a crocodile on land.
A crocodile can drag a dog in water.

— Chanakya

For his own good, a weak adversary will never contemplate a hostile act against a strong enemy, knowing such an act will result in certain ruin. A moth that flies into a flame gets burnt, the flame itself burns undisturbed.

— *Panchtantra*

A fortress is a stronghold if it has an escape route. Without one, it is just a trap.

— *Panchtantra*

One should offer to one enemy that which is likely to be taken by force by another enemy.

— Chanakya

When an aggressor is on the point of attacking, the weak king has three choices:

- He can make peace and try to avert the attack by diplomacy, or wage secret warfare.
- He can try to win over the sections favourable to himself in the aggressor's ranks by means of conciliation and gifts.
- He can prevent treachery in his own camp by sowing dissension and use of force.

— *Arthaśāstra*

There are four kinds of war:

- War by counsel, namely the exercise of diplomacy — this applies mainly when a king finds himself in a weaker position and considers it unwise to engage in battle.
- Open warfare, specifying time and place.
- Concealed warfare, or psychological warfare, including instigation of treachery in the enemy ranks.
- Clandestine war which uses covert methods to achieve the objective without actually waging a battle, usually by assassinating the enemy. In waging clandestine war, the king uses not only his own agents and double agents, but also allies, vassal kings, tribal chiefs and suborned friends and supporters of the enemy.

— *Arthaśāstra*

The king who wants to defeat a wicked, hasty, lazy or short sighted enemy, must create a false sense of confidence by making a treaty without any conditions about territory, period or objective but one merely an affirmation of an alliance. Under cover of the treaty, the king must find out the weak points of the enemy, and then strike.

— *Arthaśāstra*

The following adversely affect the efficient functioning of the army:

- Not giving due honours;
- Not paying regular salaries;
- Lack of rest after a long march;
- Exhaustion after a battle;
- Depletion in numbers;
- Suffering a set-back;
- Defeat in a frontal battle;
- Fighting in an unsuitable terrain;
- Low morale;
- Abandonment by a commander;
- Traitors in the rank;
- Anger and disunity;
- Being cut off from supplies and reinforcements;
- Demobilization and dispersal;
- Additional threat by an army from the rear flanks; and
- Lack of leadership.

— *Arthaśāstra*

A king shall engage in a declared open fight when his army is superior, or his instigation in the enemy's camp has been successful and all precautions against dangers have been taken, or the terrain is suitable to him.

— *Arthaśāstra*

A king should use deception and the enemy should be attacked when his forces are suffering from a crisis, or when his forces are unprotected or he is on less suitable terrain.

— *Arthaśāstra*

If the aggressor sets out in despite efforts to avert the attack, a weaker king must sue for peace.

— *Arthaśāstra*

The three kinds of war are open war, secret war, and undeclared war:

- Open war is fighting at a specified time and place;
- Secret war is terrorizing, sudden assault, threatening in one direction while attacking in another, sudden assault without specifying time or place, attacking an enemy when he makes a mistake or is suffering from a crisis, and appearing to yield in one place but attacking suddenly in another;
- Undeclared war is using secret agents and occult practices against the enemy.

— *Arthaśāstra*

Peace with a more powerful king carries great danger for kings, except when one is actually at war with an enemy.

— *Arthaśāstra*

A king can achieve progress by waging war if:

- He is confident of repelling an enemy attack because of having a superior forces such as martial races and fighting guilds;
- He has impregnable defences, such as a mountain, forest or river fort with only one approach;
- He can destroy the enemy's undertakings from the security of an impregnable fort on the border of his kingdom;
- The enemy's undertakings are on the verge of collapse, having been weakened by a crisis, or a part of the enemy's country can be absorbed while he is busy fighting elsewhere.

— *Arthaśāstra*

A king can achieve progress without waging war or suing for peace if:

- Neither the king nor his enemy can ruin each other's undertakings; or
- If the enemy is involved in a calamity or a life and death struggle permitting the king to concentrate on augmenting his own resources.

— *Arthaśāstra*

When total destruction is imminent, a wise man sacrifices half and works with the rest; for a complete loss is unbearable.

— *Panchtantra*

A king shall make peace with the enemy when:

- He and the enemy both achieve equal progress in equal time;
- Both decline equally in equal time; or
- There is no change in their respective situations during the same period of time.

— *Arthaśāstra*

A conqueror, having assured himself about his superiority in power, place and time, shall first leave behind a third or a quarter of his army to protect his capital, the rear, the forest regions and the borders. He shall then march towards the enemy taking with him enough wealth and forces to help him achieve his objective.

— *Arthaśāstra*

If there are two strong kings from whom protection can be sought, a king shall choose the one more capable or the one for whom he is a buffer, or both. If allied with both, the king shall plead helplessness and help neither but sow dissension between them by carrying tales that each was plotting to attack the other. When they are divided, he shall promote discord between them and then eliminate them one by one by covert methods.

— *Arthaśāstra*

A conqueror, or the enemy, having consolidated his power, may so weaken himself with uncontrolled enjoyment and dissipation as to be easily overpowered. Or, he may adopt wrong tactics such as isolating himself with all his forces in a place that is easily attacked.

— *Arthaśāstra*

The kind of people easily subverted by the enemy are the angry, the greedy, the frightened and the haughty.

— *Arthaśāstra*

The enemy, however strong he may be, becomes vulnerable to harassment and destruction when he is squeezed between the conqueror and his allies.

— *Arthaśāstra*

Ever victorious and ever unconquered shall be that warrior who is nurtured by knowledge, made prosperous by the counsel of able ministers, and has as his weapons, the precepts of warfare.

— *Arthaśāstra*

No enemy should know the king's secrets. The king shall, however, know all his enemy's weaknesses. Like a tortoise, he shall draw in any limb of his that is exposed.

— *Arthaśāstra*

The three components of power are economic strength, military might and enthusiasm in that order. A king who is superior, these components overcomes his adversary.

— *Arthaśāstra*

There are three possibilities:

- Treason wholly within the constituents of a state;
- Treachery instigated by the enemy; and
- Enemy instigated treachery compounded by internal treason.

— *Arthaśāstra*

A hunter captures a bird using another bird.
In the same way, to destroy enemies,
first offer a bait and create trust.

— Chanakya

We rarely pause to reflect on the final outcome when we are in hot pursuit of something. Bees leave blossoming flowers to sit behind an elephant's ears, oblivious of what will happen when the elephant flaps the ears.

— *Panchtantra*

As flowing streams erode mountains,
the tricks of the cunning can wear out even the best minds.

— *Panchtantra*

Self Control

Stay silent if you have to
but don't be abrasive or rude in your response.
— Chanakya

He who talks of other's faults, exposes his own shortcomings and insecurities.
— Chanakya

The wise don't waste time
on what is not achievable.
Or on what is gone.
Or lose their calm when faced with problems.
— *Hitopadeśa*

Just as sea cannot be heated
by a burning flame,
a wise man does not get agitated
even when provoked.
— *Hitopadeśa*

Most men go into a daze and cannot think clearly when faced with adversity.
— *Panchtantra*

A person who can remain calm even in a crisis is sure to cross the river of life safely and enjoy happiness.

— *Panchtantra*

An ill-directed mind can do more damage than the worst enemy.

— *Sutta Pitaka*

A well directed mind will do us greater service than a mother, a father, or any relative.

— *Sutta Pitaka*

One who succumbs to anger without ascertaining the real truth will be extremely sorry.

— *Hitopadeśa*

Anyone who can control anger, lust, arrogance, pride and greed, will find happiness.

— *Hitopadeśa*

Success and fortune select those who reflect before embarking on a course of action. Catastrophe selects those who act arrogantly and impulsively.

— *Hitopadeśa*

Self-control is acquired by giving up lust, anger, greed, conceit, arrogance and foolhardiness.

— *Arthaśāstra*

In all dealings with royalty,
with gods and teachers,
with children and the elderly,
with clerics and the unwell,
anger should be kept at bay.
— *Hitopadeśa*

Not collecting revenues when due,
embezzlement of money,
a lack of focus and integrity,
and a love of pleasures
are faults that destroy
men and leaders alike.
— *Hitopadeśa*

Words uttered without reason,
or without regard to the place or time,
or without consideration to their value or benefit,
or unpleasant words;
all lower us in other's estimation.
They are not words but poison.
— *Panchtantra*

A wise man,
even when endowed with strength and power
will not make enemies.
What man of sense will for no reason swallow poison,
thinking why not,
my physician can neutralize its effects.
— *Panchtantra*

A secure and strong person
should never insult others in public.
Or make statements that cause others distress,
even when the statements are true.

— *Panchtantra*

Exercise self control.
Anger will destroy you.

— Chanakya

You cannot accomplish your goals by being rash and impulsive.

— Chanakya

Control over your senses is the essence of all learning in the sciences and the scriptures.

— Chanakya

If one lusts after women, then one loses the advantages . . . . It is the same with drinking: loss of one's senses, loss of health, separation from good people, association with bad ones, excessive indulgence in music and singing, throwing away one's wealth as well as loss of learning, intellect, strength and good friends.

— *Arthaśāstra*

Excessive desire leads to the cultivation of evil things,
while anger causes the abandonment of good things.
Both result in a multitude of evils.

— *Arthaśāstra*

Good living requires avoiding over-indulgence in all pleasures of the senses, namely hearing, touch, sight, taste and smell.

— *Arthaśāstra*

As an archer steadies his arrow,
so a wise man steadies his trembling thoughts
which are difficult to guard and difficult to hold back.

— *Sutta Pitaka* (Buddhist Scriptures)

He who lives looking for pleasures alone,
his senses uncontrolled,
without moderation in his food,
idle and weak,
temptation will overthrow him,
just as the wind throws down a weak tree.

— *Sutta Pitaka* (Buddhist Scriptures)

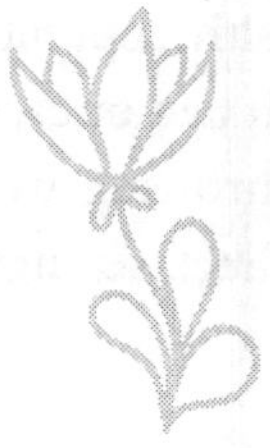

Strategy

You can beat a foe by cunning
even where force fails.
— *Panchtantra*

Don't speak what will not be believed
even if it is the truth.
— Chanakya

When the loss of one's wealth
and danger to life is imminent,
(the ruler) should bow to the enemy
and protect his life and wealth.
— Chanakya

Depending on the circumstance,
enter into an alliance with an enemy
and fight a war with friends.
The wise let go relationships
if it is for a purpose or to achieve a goal.
— Chanakya

Win over a miser with wealth,
the proud with respect,
fools by flattery and the learned with truth.
— Chanakya

Just as the hunter subdues the elephant,
the wise always triumphs over the brave.
— Chanakya

During the day, the crow can kill the owl.
At night, the owl can kill the crow.
Pick the time and place of your fight
carefully.
— Chanakya

Sign a treaty of peace
with those better or equal to you
and fight those who are inferior.
— Chanakya

Don't go to war against the mighty.
Clouds don't go against the direction of the wind.
— *Hitopadeśa*

What you can achieve by tact,
can never be achieved by war.
— *Hitopadeśa*

While extreme effort may be required
for ultimate success,
'tis best to begin with small steps.
— *Panchtantra*

Weapons are rarely enough to bring down an enemy.
T'is strategy that finally brings his doom.
Strategy strikes at an enemy's heart,
destroying his fame and sovereignty.

— *Panchtantra*

A man who has his back to the wall
will use his presence of mind and intelligence
and resort to whatever means that serve his interest,
whether they are noble or mean.

— *Panchtantra*

Like a fox,
a shrewd person accomplishes his own good
and an enemy's downfall
by playing his cards close to his chest
and not giving any hint of his aims.

— *Panchtantra*

A wise man knows
it's time to withdraw rather than fight
when loss is certain or there are no gains to be made.

— *Panchtantra*

Suppress your enemies and diseases at the very beginning.
Or they will become strong and destroy you.

— *Panchtantra*

What you cannot achieve by force and bravery,
can be achieved by strategy and intelligence.
— *Hitopadeśa*

Who in his right mind
will stake himself and his rule,
his allies, arms and reputation
upon the many oscillations
— the balance of which is never clear —
if one ends up in a war.
— *Hitopadeśa*

When you are staring destruction in its face,
make peace with even the base,
for in such times
without their sanctuary,
even the noble ones are in jeopardy
-- *Hitopadeśa*

Power, place and time are interdependent.
A powerful king can overcome the difficulties
of dry or wet terrain
and the effects of heat, cold or rain.
A dog on land can pull a crocodile
while in water a crocodile can pull in a dog
and so place is important.
Some others hold time to be the most important.
A crow can kill an owl during the day
while an owl can kill crow at night.
— *Arthaśāstra*

A conqueror must judge the relative strengths and weakness of the following aspects — both his and his adversary's — before starting on a military expedition:

- power;
- the place of engagement;
- the time of the military engagement;
- the right time to mobilize different types of forces;
- the possibility of revolts and rebellions in the rear;
- the likely losses, expenses and gains; and
- the likely dangers.

If, on balance, after giving due weight to the different factors, the conqueror is superior, a campaign can be undertaken; otherwise not.

— *Arthaśāstra*

Placating with gifts involves the giving away of land wealth and girls, and the promise of security, and freedom from fear of being overthrown.

— *Arthaśāstra*

Dissension is sown by demanding wealth, troops, land or inheritance from a subjugated king on behalf of a neighbouring king, a jungle thief, a protector or an unjustly treated prince of the subjugated king's family.

– *Arthaśāstra*

If there is no strong king whose protection can be sought against the enemy, it is better to make peace with the enemy.

— *Arthaśāstra*

The king can achieve progress by making peace with his enemy if he thinks that he can use the period of peace such that:

- his gain through productive undertakings would be so great as to enable him to destroy those of the enemy;
- he can enjoy the additional gain from his own works (not spent in waging war) or those arising from works undertaken by the enemy or those accruing from the confidence generated by the peace;
- he can ruin the enemy's undertakings by using secret methods or occult practices;
- he can entice away the people implementing the enemy's projects by offering them higher remuneration, favours or remissions of taxes;
- the enemy, being allied with a much stronger king, will undergo a decline;
- he can manage to prolong the war between the enemy and another king;
- he can acquire parts of the enemy's territory attacked by another and thereby gain the profits of the enemy's undertakings;
- he can harass the countryside of another of his enemies;
- he can be safe from attack by the enemy who finds himself in a difficult situation due to the destruction of his undertakings;
- he can expect to improve his situation to start

profitable undertakings elsewhere with another king;

- he can sow dissension between the enemy and the enemy's allies and make them his own allies; and
- he can, by a judicious use of favours and punishments, make the enemy's own allies turn against him and eventually destroy him.

— *Arthaśāstra*

A king may agree to forego a large immediate gain and seek only a small future benefit:

- if it helps his ally and harms his enemy while maintaining his own advantage; or
- if he intends to use again the partner who is being helped by asking for very little benefit.

— *Arthaśāstra*

When a king at war with another finds that the enemy's principal constituents — though greedy, impoverished and rebellious — do not come over to his side for fear of the war, he shall make peace even if he is the stronger of the two. At the least he shall reduce the intensity of the war.

— *Arthaśāstra*

A king shall adopt a dual policy if he can promote his own undertakings by having peace with one enemy and, at the same time, ruin those of another foe by waging war.

— *Arthaśāstra*

He shall not wage war against a stronger king because he who fights against a stronger king is crushed like a foot soldier fighting an elephant. A fight with an equal brings losses to both sides, just like the destruction of two unbaked clay pots hitting each other.

— *Arthaśāstra*

The six methods of dealing with adversaries are:
making peace, waging war, doing neither,
preparing for war, seeking protection
and adopting a dual policy.

— *Anonymous*

When the benefits accruing to kings under a treaty, irrespective of their status as the weaker, equal or stronger king, is fair to each one, peace by agreement shall be the preferred course. If the benefits are to be distributed unfairly, war is preferable.

— *Arthaśāstra*

A king shall try to win over secretly any one who can start a revolt or can put one down. He shall approach one who is true to his word, capable of helping the king in achieving his objectives or of saving him from difficulties. He shall first form a judgment about whether the man is upright or a villain.Upright men conspire for the sake of others similarly placed while villains do so only for their own benefit.

— *Arthaśāstra*

The king shall make a treaty with an upright ruler,
but with a villain a treaty shall be made with a view to
outmaneuvering him.

—*Arthaśāstra*

Don't disregard your foe or your health.
Whoever allows them to march unchecked,
will soon meet his end.

— *Panchtantra*

A clever mind will succeed
where brute force fails to accomplish results.

— *Hitopadeśa*

A mirage makes desert look like water;
So, too, an enemy can look like a friend.

— Chanakya

Water seeps in gradually into a leaking boat,
eventually sinking it.
An enemy slips in from the smallest chink
and works his way to cause total ruin.

— *Panchtantra*

To disunite the enemy using his own kin is the best strategy. Put all efforts in setting up a rival insider when pitted against a foe.

— *Hitopadeśa*

A king may not seek any benefit in the present or in the future if:

- He wants to save another king engaged in a war with traitors or enemies or with a stronger king threatening his territory;
- He wants the other king to come to his help in similar circumstances; or
- He takes into account a special relationship with the other king.

— *Arthaśāstra*

Where persuasion and gifts don't work,
try intrigue.
It rarely fails.

— *Panchtantra*

Even when a king is facing financial difficulties or when he distrusts the other partner in negotiations, he may accept a small immediate gain for the sake of a large future benefit, when he wants:

- To make the enemy, whose undertakings had not started well, suffer further losses or expenses;
- To prevent the success of the enemy's undertakings, which had started well;
- To attack the enemy's base camp, heartland or expedition; or
- To extract more benefit later after making a treaty with the enemy of the other partner.

— *Arthaśāstra*

If a king is unable to ruin the enemy's undertakings and is also unable to protect his own from the enemy's attacks, he shall seek the help of a stronger king. Under this protection he shall first avert his decline and then move towards progress.

— *Arthaśāstra*

When loss of the whole is imminent,
the prudent part with a half,
and carry on with the other half,
for a total loss is hard to bear.

— *Panchtantra*

Men with commonsense will not spend too much for too little profit. Prudence means protecting a great deal at little expense.

— *Panchtantra*

Don't charge against a strong foe if you are weak.
Just like an elephant with broken tusks,
you are sure to beat a hasty retreat.

— *Hitopadeśa*

Make peace with an enemy
who is as strong as you are.
In a battle between equals, victory hangs in the balance.
Never fight unless you are sure of success.

— *Panchtantra*

’Tis best not to trust someone whose strength,
background and conduct are not known.
— *Panchtantra*

If no gain is expected, why fight a war?
— *Panchtantra*

Try to make peace with an enemy by gifts
or create dissidence.
But try and avoid war.
— *Hitopadeśa*

Success

Success and failure are common to all paths.
— Chanakya

Success can be achieved by endeavour
and never by wish alone.
A lion's jaws are never visited by the passing deer.
— *Hitopadeśa*

Falling for feminine grace,
being partial to your family and friends,
laziness, diffidence and ill health,
are six things that will impede success.
— *Hitopadeśa*

Though ultimate success may result from extreme
effort, the beginning should be marked by small steps.
— *Panchtantra*

Success is rarely won by those
who are rash in taking risks
or those who are indecisive
but by those who combine prudence with bravery.
— *Hitopadeśa*

When a man's star is on the rise,
his intellectual capacity begins to grow,
memory becomes sharp,
opportunities seem to offer themselves on a platter,
counsel rarely flounders,
judgement reflects the promise of success,
the mind attains new heights,
and the man basks in doing good deeds.

— *Panchtantra*

One who conquers himself
is better than the greatest of conquerors.
Not even god can reverse the victory of a man
who has conquered himself.

— *Sutta Pitaka*

Success does not care to knock at the doors of those
who lack ambition or initiative, or are lazy or fatalistic.

— *Hitopadeśa*

Success will touch those who are fearless
irrespective of the battlefield.
And those who are equally at ease
in their home town or abroad.

— *Hitopadeśa*

Just as a river can equally submerge both grass
and trees,
the skilled can do big and small things with
the same ease.

— *Hitopadeśa*

Passion, anger, timidity,
compassion which leads to aversion to fighting,
recoiling from awarding deserved punishment,
baseness, haughtiness, a forgiving nature, being too
pious, meanness, abjectness, jealousy,
contempt for what one has,
wickedness, distrust, fear, negligence,
inability to withstand harsh climate — cold, heat or rain
— and faith in the auspiciousness of stars and days
are all obstacles to achievement.

— *Arthasastra*

Teamwork & Unity

Just as a rope woven out of straw
can hold an elephant,
a team can deliver
even if its members are individually weak.

— *Panchtantra*

The birds may fly away with my net.
But as soon as they break away,
I wrest all the power.

— *Hitopadeśa*

The man who will not listen to what his well wishing teammates say, his misfortunes are drawing near as foes are on their way.

— *Hitopadeśa*

Just as an elephant is unable to snap a rope woven out of straw, a group of people will always win when they work together.

— *Hitopadeśa*

Rice separated from husk will never ripen and grow golden.

— *Hitopadeśa*

As with thick and thorny bamboo shoot,
which in clusters are impossible to uproot,
so it is with those who stand
as a team in a close knit band.
— *Hitopadeśa*

Good qualities will get hidden
if you surround yourself with fools.
Even the sun loses its shine
when hidden by clouds.
— Chanakya

Just like you cannot uproot bamboos
when they are in a cluster.
You cannot breach a team that holds together.
— *Hitopadeśa*

A heroic lone man is an easy prey
for foes who gang up to destroy him.
— *Panchtantra*

Trust & Friendship

Putting your trust in friends who are evil, fickle false or foolish is worse than sharing your home with enemies, or walking with a snake.

— *Hitopadeśa*

Gain trust first. Even gods can't beat their enemies without first gaining their trust.

— *Panchtantra*

Wise men cannot place their trust in rulers, women, snakes, their own knowledge, in war, fire and evil men.

— Chanakya

Keep neither proximity with, nor distance from, rulers, fire, teachers and women. Both can spell disaster.

— Chanakya

In distress, you realize who your family really is.
Only in war, do you realize who are really brave.
When money runs low,
you realize how loyal your wife is.
And in emergencies you realize who your friends are.

— *Hitopadeśa*

Don't trust creatures with claws and horns.
Neither trust kings nor men who bear arms
or who have feminine charms.

— *Hitopadeśa*

A man who turns friendly after being nasty cannot be trusted.

— *Panchtantra*

Don't trust a man who cannot be trusted,
nor trust a trustworthy man beyond a point.
Too much trust is dangerous
and can result in ruin.

— *Panchtantra*

There is no man in this world
who does not succumb to
subordinates who go out of the way to please him,
guests who fill him up with flattery,
women who drown him in their crocodile tears,
and mentors who he looks up to.

— *Panchtantra*

Don't trust a defeated enemy who has now become a friend. A crow does not venture into a smoke-filled cave even if the fire has been put out.

— Chanakya

Don't trust good or bad friends with secrets. An angered friend, whether good or bad, is capable of disclosing all your secrets.

— Chanakya

A true friend stands by you
in happiness and sadness,
in times of anarchy,
in a court of law and the cemetery.

— *Hitopadeśa*

A friend is someone who you can trust
like you trust your mother
Others are acquaintances
specially when you fear their anger
Or don't know where you stand with them.

— *Hitopadeśa*

An able, skilled, bold, energetic man
can achieve little if he has no friends.
A fire lit with a few twigs dies out on its own.

— *Panchtantra*

A person should always look for new friends
if he plans to rise high.
In spite of being full, an ocean waits eagerly
for the water from rivers to flow into it.

— *Panchtantra*

You must be able to trust a friend
like you trust your mother.
Friends whose anger you fear,
or whose words concern you,
or a friend with whom
you don't know where you stand,
is not a friend but an acquaintance.
— *Panchtantra*

We are two birds of the same family.
I was brought up well
and you in bad company.
I hear good things
and you street language.
It is association that breeds vice or virtue in us.
— *Panchtantra*

Friends and foes can be discerned by observing who helps and who causes hindrances.
— *Hitopadeśa*

A man needs to act with candour with the gods,
with himself and his mentor.
With all others, double dealing is best.
— *Panchtantra*

No one is born a friend or enemy;
conduct and behaviour decide this.
— *Hitopadeśa*

For success, 'tis important that we have
many friends of every mould.
Pigeons need a mouse to gnaw the net
when they are trapped in it.

— *Hitopadeśa*

Giving and receiving,
listening to and telling secrets,
entertaining and being entertained,
are the six indicators of friendship.

— *Panchtantra*

Wealth

It's not the loss of wealth that makes me sad,
for wealth will return.
It's the way friends disappear when I run out of money.

— *Panchtantra*

Opulence perverts the mind.
In the end, wealth will always blind men.

— *Hitopadeśa*

Trying to accomplish anything without any resources or capital is like trying to plough through sand.

— Chanakya

Seek wealth with indifference to it and for good causes.
'Tis better to stay away from mud than to clean its stains.

— *Hitopadeśa*

It is natural to desire wealth.
There is no greater misery than not having it.

— *Hitopadeśa*

You are the master and wealth is the servant if you stop craving for it. But give in to its temptation and servitude is at your door.

— *Hitopadeśa*

Once you get what you long for,
a new wish list will take over.
Try and live with what you have
and the wish list itself will recede.
— *Hitopadeśa*

Wealth brings strength and wisdom.
It gives stature in life.
— *Hitopadeśa*

He who is conned into parting with his money is a fool.
— *Panchtantra*

The world does not respect even gods they have no wealth.
— Chanakya

The world functions for the sake of money.
— Chanakya

After creating wealth,
turn your attention to charity and integrity.
Wealth is like us —
transitory, perishable in a moment.
— Chanakya

The wealthy buy beauty through gifts,
strength through servants, respect through entertaining,
lineage through marrying into influential families.
— Chanakya

Wealth is a king's friend
in forging treaties in war,
in philanthropy,
in winning fame, in winning happiness
and in attaining and remaining in power.

— Chanakya

Virtues and pleasures depend on wealth.
Wealth enriches and enhances life.

— Chanakya

Wealth is unmatched beauty,
wealth is auspicious,
wealth is bursting youth,
wealth is life itself.

— Chanakya

Qualities are attained by wealth, not wealth by qualities.
The wealthy are served by those with good qualities,
not vice versa.

— Chanakya

The old, the famous, the learned, the skilled, the brave, the clergy, poets and noble men all have this to say to a rich man, "May you be victorious! May you live long!"

— Chanakya

Where does it come come from?
Where does it go?
It is impossible to figure our wealth's path.

— Chanakya

Friends, wives, relatives desert men without wealth only to return when they again become rich. Wealth is man's only real friend.

— Chanakya

Swans stay where there is water. They abandon it when water dries up and come back when there is water. Men should not replicate such behaviour.

— Chanakya

To succeed, men need wealth.
Just as elephants are needed
to capture more wild elephants.

— Chanakya

Wealth accumulated through illegal or unethical means lasts for ten years. In the eleventh year it's completely lost.

— Chanakya

Wealth is meant to be spent, not stored.

— Chanakya

A wealthy man who lets his wealth sit idle
is nothing but a fool performing a guard's work.
— *Panchtantra*

Wealth has no place for those who consult the stars.
Wealth is its own star. What can the stars or skies do?
— Chanakya

Man is not a slave of man, but of money.
Wealth or poverty decides whether he is great
or a nobody.
Hitopadeśa

First, wealth is difficult to obtain,
guarding it is then a strain.
losing it is a bit like death,
it's better not to think of that at all.
— *Hitopadeśa*

Human beings live in fear of death.
But the wealthy live in constant fear
of flood and fire,
of thieves and kings,
and even of their near and dear.
— *Hitopadeśa*

Animals are preyed upon on land
and birds preyed upon in the sky.
Fish get preyed upon on in water.
The rich are preyed upon everywhere.
— *Hitopadeśa*

Wealth requires pain to acquire
and in troubled times, leads to anxiety
In affluence, it causes some strange delusion.
Can it really be a cause for comfort?
— *Hitopadeśa*

Wealth shares the same characteristic as
a passing cloud's shadow,
young women and false friends.
All are transient in their nature.
— *Hitopadeśa*

Why be proud when you are rich today
and lament when wealth has gone?
Men are like a ball in play,
up one day and down another.
— *Hitopadeśa*

His senses, mind and name are still the same.
Yet he lacks the glow that comes from affluence.
Without wealth, a man transforms into someone he is not.
— *Hitopadeśa*

Lack of wealth invites shame
and shame reduces confidence.
Without confidence,
you invite contempt.
Contempt invites depression and a loss of intelligence
which is sure to lead to destruction.

— *Hitopadeśa*

It is the rich who have the power.
That's always been the universal fact.
That much is clear even in the king's dominion.

— *Hitopadeśa*

Just as frogs seek wells
and birds a lake with water.
Wealth looks for enterprising men.

— *Panchtantra*

Wealth seeks a man of substance,
who is prompt and diligent,
firm on his word
and undeterred by misfortune.

— *Panchtantra*

Virtue, integrity, kindness, modesty,
good nature and noble birth,
all lose their shine and worth
when a man loses his wealth.

— *Panchtantra*

Wit, kindness and modesty,
pleasantness and beauty,
liveliness and vitality,
happiness and humour,
integrity and knowledge,
wisdom and purity,
respect for rules and right conduct;
all these fine attributes are found in the wealthy.

— *Panchtantra*

There is nothing in this world
that wealth cannot accomplish.
So let the sole aim of men be making money.

— *Panchtantra*

A man's strengths might be grounded in justice
but if he has no money,
his employer hates him even if he provides good service,
his family leaves him high and dry,
his wife grows cold and distanced,
good friends shun his sight,
His virtues cease to glow and miseries continue to grow.

— *Panchtantra*

Prosperity does not care to grant favours to the lazy and those without enterprise.

— *Hitopadeśa*

Even the minds of men with intellect
start to decay
when deprived of wealth and power,
and preoccupied with nagging problems
of supporting their families.

— *Panchtantra*

Lack of wealth makes men weak,
insignificant and beneath notice.
Like bubbles that form and dissolve on streams.

— *Panchtantra*

A fool is tormented by thoughts like, "These sons belong to me, and this wealth belongs to me." Where is the chance of wealth belonging to him when he himself does not belong to himself.

— *Sutta Pitaka*

My wealth has been enjoyed,
my dependents supported,
protected from contingencies by me.
I have provided for charity, too.
For whatever aim a person would desire wealth,
that aim I have achieved.
I have done what will not lead to future distress.

— Anguttara Nikaya in *Adiya Sutta*

How can men running after wealth find time to be content.

— *Panchtantra*

If you are satisfied with whatever wealth you have
and consider it a treasure trove,
then you already have all you deserve
and will get no more.
— *Hitopadeśa*

Money is troublesome to earn,
even more troublesome to guard.
Getting it, or spending it, brings unhappiness.
Money is a curse.
— *Panchtantra*

The riches of the world are never without enemies;
he who possesses them resembles a tree laden with
fruit.
— *Theravada Buddhism*

A wise man uses his wits to make money
but avoids being a miser;
for he may be destined to lose his money.
The art is in learning how to enjoy it.
— *Panchtantra*

Quick in spending and never taking measure,
such a man will lose his wealth no matter how rich he is.
— *Hitopadeśa*

A man who lets wealth
that good fortune showers on him sit idle,
finds no happiness in this world, nor in the next.
He is a fool doing a watchman's job
— *Hitopadeśa*

With men of dim intelligence
and lacking wealth to boot,
all undertakings fail and get lost
as little streams in summer do.
— *Panchtantra*

Men without wealth are like dried corn and wild seeds;
all without substance and unproductive.
— *Panchtantra*

Wealth magnifies a man's virtues.
Just like the sun illuminates the world.
— *Panchtantra*

Without wealth, friends and family have no time;
self esteem takes a beating; misfortunes swell and multiply;
and others find everything wrong with you.
— *Panchtantra*

Desire for wealth is not a vice.
— Chanakya

Prosperity will leave those who are satisfied with the wealth they have.

— Chanakya

Acquisition of wealth has its root in wealth.

— Chanakya

Wealth is a prerequisite for righteousness and pleasures.

— Chanakya

Fortune follows effort.

— Chanakya

Endless effort and struggle may not bring the wealth you desire. But if it has to come, then nothing will stop it from coming.

— *Panchtantra*

Strive to get something you don't have as yet;
and when you get it, guard it so
that it continues to grow.
And once it has grown,
give it away to those who need it most.

— *Hitopadeśa*

Knowledge and wealth are accumulated bit by bit;
much as drops of water fill up a pitcher.

— *Hitopadeśa*

Material wealth alone can help you enjoy pleasures
and gain respect.
— Chanakya

The stubborn forfeit fame,
the irritable lose friends,
those who focus only on work,
lose their families.
Obsession with money kills virtues,
being miserly destroys peace of mind.
— *Panchtantra*

Wealth will slip away from that childish man
who constantly consults the stars.
The only guiding star of wealth is wealth itself;
what can the stars of the sky do?
— *Arthaśāstra*

The value of land is what man makes of it.
— *Arthaśāstra*

A man gains great wealth by emulating the flexible reed,
rather than by having the overbearing nature of a snake.
—*Panchtantra*

You can gain respect and glory
even if you are not wealthy.
But there is no respect or glory
for a wealthy miser.
—*Hitopadeśa*

Rivers find their end in oceans.
Family ties find their end in feuds of women.
Secrets find their end in gossip.
Family fortunes find their end in incompetent sons.
— *Panchtantra*

Just as chains cannot hold a drunk elephant, wealth will never be able to confine the wise.
— *Hitopadeśa*

Those who specialize in buying and selling
and those who travel to distant lands to trade,
multiply their fortune.
— *Panchtantra*

A man preoccupied with wealth, gives up values and lets go his family, abandons his birthplace and goes to foreign lands.
— *Panchtantra*

The deeper you dig to bury your gold,
the closer you come to misery.
— *Hitopadeśa*

Wealth without happiness
is like carrying someone else's burden and suffering.
— *Hitopadeśa*

When a man is faced with waning fortune, friends shy away and the affectionate turn cold.

— *Panchtantra*

Separate a man from his wealth
and he finds his senses numbed.
Even though he continues to speak the same way,
and has the same intelligent mind,
he does not remain the same person.

— *Panchtantra*

A man with no money feels shame.
Covered with shame, he finds his spirit stripped.
Without the motivation, he is easily defeated.
With repeated defeats, he goes into depression.
In depression, sadness overtakes him.
Sadness dims his intelligence.
Without intelligence, his efforts bear no results.
Poverty, ladies and gentlemen, is at the root of all evils.

— *Panchtantra*

One who guards even a pice from being wrongly spent as if it were a hoard of gold, but is willing to spend millions when the situation demands, and that too with an open hand, prosperity will never leave his hand.

— *Hitopadeśa*

Those they serve others for the sake of money
cannot even preserve their own freedom.

— *Hitopadeśa*

For wealth the foolish can behave like whores.
And make themselves a puppet in the hands of others.
— *Hitopadeśa*

Wealth protects righteousness,
practice protects learning,
good rule protects a ruler,
and good women protect a home.
— Chanakya

Fools let go of greater revenues fearing a small expense.
Would a man with any sense
give up income because of the tax he must bear.
— *Hitopadeśa*

Trees with fragrance also attract snakes.
Lakes may be home to lilies but also attract crocodiles.
Life will bring happiness but will also bring sadness.
Prosperity cannot come entirely free of problems.
— *Hitopadeśa*

You tend to get more cuts
where there is already a wound.
You feel hungrier than usual when you are short of money.
— *Panchtantra*

The implementation of all programs of the ruler
depends on the resources of the treasury.
— Chanakya

A man who does not measure his wealth regularly
or spends it for pleasure
Will face eventually poverty
even though he may be as rich
as the goddess of wealth.
— *Hitopadeśa*

For weddings and emergencies,
for loyal friends and a woman one loves,
for the welfare of family and children,
for becoming famous or weakening enemies,
there is no such thing as overspending.
— *Hitopadeśa*

Wisdom

Which bad employee is not guilty of bad work?
Who living on bad food will not fall sick?
Who does fortune not make forget humility?
Who does death not end the cycle for?
Who addicted to pleasure and comfort
does not burn with pain and sorrow?

— *Panchtantra*

Don't pit your strength against a mob;
'tis hard to win against a crowd.
An army of red ants can eat up a big snake.

— *Hitopadeśa*

A murderer, a drunkard, an impotent,
a traitor, or a man who does not keep his promise
can always atone for his mistakes.
There is no atonement for an ungrateful person.

— *Panchtantra*

No one has everything.
Gold has no fragrance, sugarcane no fruit,
sandalwood has no flower, a scholar no wealth
and a ruler rarely has a long life.

— Chanakya

A king is ruined by bad advice;
an ascetic by bad company;
a child by indulgence;
an intellectual by lack of learning;
a noble line by lazy sons;
good conduct by serving the cunning;
friendship by lack of respect;
investment by mismanagement;
affection by long absence;
a woman by drink;
a farm by neglect;
and wealth by senseless spending.

— *Panchtantra*

A dispute between equals is understandable;
as one between the wealthy and the powerful.
But a dispute between the great and small
is beyond comprehension.

— *Hitopadeśa*

Just like a river flows ever forward,
there is nothing to be achieved by looking back in life.

— *Hitopadeśa*

Throughout history, kings and nobles did many great and heroic deeds, yet there is no trace of their good work. Time obliterates everything.

— *Hitopadeśa*

Snakes haunt scented forests.
Crocodiles lurk below lakes floating with lotus.
Rogues are everywhere seeking to destroy virtue.
Happiness never comes without its mix of trouble.
— *Panchtantra*

Shun a friend who flatters in your presence
but criticizes you behind your back.
He is nothing but a glass of milk laced with poison.
— *Panchtantra*

Other than fire, five things burn us:
serving a bad ruler,
being in debt,
disgrace in front of our friends and family,
separation from one we love, and
friends that turns away when we need them
or when we have no money.
— Chanakya

The birds abandon the tree when there are no fruits, swans abandon the dried up lake, women abandon men who are no longer rich, ministers abandon a fallen ruler, bees abandon a wilted flower, animals a burnt forest. People try to please others for some selfish motive. Who rules over whom?
— Chanakya

Fools and fish,
women and crab,
lime and indigo,
and drunks
hold fast and won't let go.
— *Panchtantra*

Who has not become arrogant with wealth?
Who has not been hurt by women?
Who has been a permanent favourite of rulers?
Who has escaped the march of age?
Which beggar can claim dignity?
Which person in bad company
has been able to live in safety?
— Chanakya

Marriage precedes disputes.
— Chanakya

What will a lion get
by digging into a rat's rocky hole?
Except for broken claws and a mouse at best.
— *Panchtantra*

Faults are common even among the learned.
— Chanakya

Rulers cannot be friends,
crows cannot be clean,
gamblers cannot be truthful,
snakes cannot be expected to forgive,
cowards cannot show valour, and
drunkards cannot be discerning.
— Chanakya

In an assembly, an enemy should not be criticized.
— Chanakya

Doing something unethical,
enmity with your own family,
rivalry with the powerful,
and giving credence to women
are four sure ways to self destruct.
— *Hitopadeśa*

Women will fall for villains.
Kings will prefer those who praise them.
The least deserving will succeed.
The miserly will get the wealth.
And rains will fall on the mountains or the sea.
All this is mostly true.
—*Hitopadeśa*

The night feels long if you cannot sleep.
A mile feels long if you are tired.
A life feels long
if you don't know where you are headed.
— *Sutta Pitaka*

A person who mingles with the bravest,
the learned and the magnanimous, becomes virtuous.
The practice of virtue brings wealth
and wealth gets glory,
and glory begets authority.
— *Panchtantra*

One can never hope to be with anything forever.
Not even with one's own body,
nor those who are dear.
— *Hitopadeśa*

As many times a person gets into relationships
that bring him pleasure.
Just as many times
is sorrow's dart sure to strike deep inside his heart.
— *Hitopadeśa*

Don't live in a place where there is no career or philanthropy, no etiquette and courtesy and no fear of the law.
— *Hitopadeśa*

Do what you will,
what is not destined will never be.
Even when it comes into your hand,
it will slip away.
But what destiny has planned,
will surely be yours.
Destiny and action go hand in hand.
The one is as much a part of the other,
as light and shade.

— *Panchtantra*

Wisdom without vanity,
valour with magnanimity,
wealth with renunciation,
are a rarity.

— *Hitopadeśa*

Crooks revile men of integrity.
Rejected suitors sneer at lovers women adore.
Cowards condemn men of courage.
Misers criticize the charitable.
The poor despise the rich.
Fools censure wise men.
That's the way of the world.

— *Panchtantra*

If a man's faith is unsteady,
if he does not know the true picture,
if his peace of mind is troubled,
his knowledge will never be perfect.
If a man's thoughts are not scattered,
if his mind is not perplexed,
if he has ceased to think of good or evil,
then there is no fear for him.

— *Sutta Pitaka*

Proud when wealthy,
depressed when down and out,
man's rise and fall is like the bounce of a ball.

— *Panchtantra*

Get up on time, fight, divide work and responsibilities, and enjoy after a good fight.

— Chanakya

A man with character and integrity finds comfort in solitude when his luck turns bad and his efforts don't deliver desired results. Men will go through unbearable pain and find unexpected pleasure, all in a single lifetime. That's how life works.

— *Hitopadeśa*

There is no reason to sink in despair. Happiness and sorrow come uninvited to everyone.

— *Panchtantra*

A mistress deserts a man
who has lost his wealth,
subjects desert a weak ruler,
birds desert a dying tree,
guests desert a house where the party has ended.
— Chanakya

In normal times,
it behoves men to be forbearing
and women to show modesty.
But it pays to be brave in combat and bold in love.
— *Hitopadeśa*

Downfall from one's place
always leads to loss of grace.
That's true of monarchs, clerics and ministers too,
and ladies fair
and even of things like teeth and hair,
not to mention the bosom's flare.
— *Hitopadeśa*

Youth, wealth, authority and a lack of discretion, each can cause trouble, especially when they come together in one man.
— *Hitopadeśa*

Wise men walk warily under all circumstances.
They appear neither elated nor depressed
in happiness or in sorrow.
— *Sutta Pitaka*

If the fear of death were to go away
by running away from war,
then leave, by all means,
and find a new place or path.
But why not stand and fight
when death is certain for every living creature?
— *Hitopadeśa*

Association decides vice and virtue in a man.
We were two birds from the same parents.
I was brought up by the wise
and my brother by crooks.
— *Panchtantra*

From the lion, a wise man should learn this:
Undertake all big and small tasks only after full preparation.
— Chanakya

From the crane, a wise man has the following qualities to learn: Being in control of one's senses and choosing the right time and place to accomplish all tasks.
— Chanakya

When they have to meet their own ends
friends may appear foes and foes appear friends.
Few of us can tell the difference though.
— *Panchtantra*

There are six qualities to be learnt from a dog:
desire for a lot,
satisfaction with even a little,
deep slumber,
alertness in sleep,
devotion to one's master
and bravery.
— Chanakya

While friends and parents naturally care for our welfare and benefit, but we must identify the reasons when someone else shows the same care.
— *Hitopadeśa*

A man who acts with candour with foes,
with so-called friends and prostitutes,
will not survive for long.
— *Panchtantra*

A king given to kindness,
a priest given to gluttony,
an ally without integrity,
an irresponsible officer,
a disobedient servant,
and men who show no gratitude
should be avoided.
— *Hitopadeśa*

The wise don't waste time on the past
or what they lost.
And that's what differentiates them from the fools.
— *Panchtantra*

He who turns his back to desires
has read and heard all
and put to practice every learning.
— *Hitopadeśa*

Fires cannot be satisfied
with all the wood in the world.
The sea can never be filled
by all the rivers flowing into it.
Death's thirst cannot be quenched
even by all the creatures on earth.
— *Hitopadeśa*

If dissent results in some being called "fools" Which of the lot is right when the entire audience is made up of intellectuals? On the other hand if every dissenting voice has brains and wit, No "fools" exist, since all alike are at par.

— Buddha as quoted in *Sutta Nipata*

A drunk and a setting sun display the same signs;
weakness of hands, anger, fading features
and a loss of power.
— *Hitopadeśa*

The coward, running away from war, guarantees his own destruction. And one whose men are insecure will face desertion in war.

— *Hitopadeśa*

Wealth not used for charity, or enjoyed as it should be;
Strength that does not put an enemy in jeopardy;
Accumulating knowledge that is not put to practice;
A person who lacks control over his senses or passions;
They don't serve the purpose they are meant for.

— *Hitopadeśa*

A careless man can never feel safe
after he commits a blunder no matter how far he runs
The shrewd and conniving have long enough arms
to reach out and drag him back.

— *Panchtantra*

People are affectionate
as long as you have something to give them.
Even a calf forgets its mother
once her milk runs dry.

— *Panchtantra*

The worth of servants is known
when they are sent on errands,
of relatives when difficulties arise,
of friends when you are in distress,
and of a wife when you are not prosperous.

— Chanakya

The fruit of ruling is command,
the fruit of learning is knowledge
and the fruit of philanthropy is satisfaction.
— Chanakya

You should not wake up the following seven if they are asleep: the ruler, the lion, the snake, the hog, the infant, a street dog and an idiot.
— Chanakya

Disregard towards the ruler results in ruin,
disregard of one's health results in death,
disregard of other's financial interest
leads to destruction of wealth.
— Chanakya

Look for family and fortune,
learning and virtue,
good looks and good health,
and good connections
in a suitable groom for your daughter.
Other things are of little consequence.
— *Panchtantra*

When age take's over and a man's hair turns white, it marks the beginning of his disgrace. Young women shun him and flee miles away as if he were a ghost.
— *Panchtantra*

When the body is shriveled and the steps falter,
when the teeth are decayed and the face wrinkled,
when sight falls and the figure is no longer trim,
the family then finds no time for conversation,
the wife pays little attention;
even the son despises the man.

— *Panchtantra*

If separation really was the cause of sorrow
instead of one's own ignorance;
then grief should increase with each passing day
rather than reduce.

— *Hitopadeśa*

Dive in the deepest oceans or fall from a hill,
fate will guard your life still,
if you have more time yet to live.

— *Hitopadeśa*

When fate is with you, you are indestructible.
But when luck is not with you,
you will be destroyed
even when you are well defended.
We may survive in a forest
but may not be able to last at home.

— *Hitopadeśa*

Pierced with arrows he survives,
but dies then from a snake bite.
No creature dies before time
nor live beyond its designated time.

— *Hitopadeśa*

The best way to deal with sudden grief is to try and not think about it.

— *Hitopadeśa*

Don't discard what has come to you on its own.
A woman desirous of making love,
showers curses if rejected.

— Chanakya

Equal attention should be given to the three kinds of wealth which are interconnected. Any one of the three, righteousness, material wealth, physical pleasures, if excessively indulged in, harms itself and the other two.

— Chanakya

Even animals can understand meanings
of words said to them.
Horses and elephants are quick to follow when ordered.
But human beings can infer even what is not said.
To know what others are thinking
needs an insightful head.

— *Hitopadeśa*

You can infer what is inside the mind from gestures,
motions, efforts, speech and facial changes.
— *Hitopadeśa*

Doctors love a man who is sick,
and officers one who has some fault.
Clever folk survive on fools,
but goodness keeps the good alive.
— *Hitopadeśa*

Birds who rule the sky, and creatures of the deepest sea,
both get caught, regardless of their locations remote.
Stretching out its deadly hand,
Time can seize you from the furthest land.
— *Hitopadeśa*

Tend to pleasure the same way as you tend to pain.
Like a turning wheel, both will come and go again.
— *Hitopadeśa*

I regret nothing and nothing astonishes me any more.
Even the gods cannot prevent what has to happen to me.
— *Panchtantra*

Trust only those
whose rise and fall is linked to your own.
— *Hitopadeśa*

One who helps you is your brother,
even though he may be a stranger.
One who harms you is just another,
even though he may be family.
Ill health hurts
even though it originates from your own body.
Herbs provide healing
even though they grow deep in forests.

— *Hitopadeśa*

The sun and moon cannot escape an eclipse.
Elephants, snakes and birds cannot escape cages.
The intelligent cannot escape poverty.
Destiny is all powerful.

— *Panchtantra*

Birds soaring high in the sky meet with danger.
Fish deep in the sea fall into the fisherman's net.
Danger's arm will stretch
and arrest you when it is time.
And neither your position nor conduct would matter.

— *Panchtantra*

Destiny joins together what is broken
and breaks what is not.
It makes things happen beyond our imagination.

— *Panchtantra*

The deer flings the trap, tears the net,
flees far into the woods, out of the reach of hunters
only to tumble into a well.
What can effort do if fate itself decides to be cruel.
— *Panchtantra*

Don't put yourself through endless thinking.
What is destined will come to your doorstep.
— *Panchtantra*

A brave man retaliates when spoken to harshly; the arrows of insult which lie embedded in the heart inflame the spirit and affect the senses.
— *Vishalaksha*

A gambler never knows how much wealth he has, tries to enjoy wealth which he does not have, and loses it before he can enjoy it.
— *Arthaśāstra*

Even the simplest home
brings more happiness than paradise.
— *Panchtantra*

The kings are gone and so are his ministers.
The beautiful woods and clusters have perished.
And gone are the lovely women;
all lost and passed away.
Stung by the biggest leveler, mortality.
— *Panchtantra*

What has to happen will happen.
What is not slated to happen, will not.
For every problem, there is a solution.
So don't think over much; catch a drink instead.

— *Hitopadeśa*

Like creepers, kings and mistresses tend to cling to people who happen to support their views, irrespective of whether these people are unread, base or unworthy.

— *Hitopadeśa* (Adaptation)

Animals perform no rite of consecration or sacred ablution to crown the lion as their king.

— *Hitopadeśa*

A vulture can spot a dead animal
from several miles above
but it fails to spot a trap when its time has come.

— *Hitopadeśa*

One who interferes in things he has no business in,
behaves like a meddling monkey
and will face death one day.

— *Hitopadeśa*

Love should abide till death
and anger should subside in moments.
While giving there must be no thought of reciprocity.
That's what makes for a good human being.

— *Hitopadeśa*

The four ends to which most of us strive,
virtue, pleasure, wealth and deliverance,
depend on good health and safety.
— *Hitopadeśa*

Without ambition, there is no success.
Without love, there is no reason to dress up.
Without learning, there is no intellect.
— *Hitopadeśa*

Just as a mother's breasts start bearing milk when a child is born, God will make provision for as long as we live.
— *Hitopadeśa*

A piece of glass can make it to a crown.
And a diamond may be placed on a toe.
It is not the diamond's fault
if it's not recognized for what it is.
— *Hitopadeśa*

The flute, the sword or the horse,
eloquence, law and mankind itself
are good or bad depending on whose hands they are in.
— *Hitopadeśa*

Just as parakeets cannot learn no matter how much they are taught, you cannot succeed in teaching those who don't have the intelligence to grasp the learning.
— *Hitopadeśa*

A horse, a weapon and a text,
a lute, a voice, a man and a woman
behave well or badly depending on who they serve.
— *Hitopadeśa*

As a hurricane snaps only tall trees
and leaves the grass alone
A strong man takes on others of equal might.
— *Hitopadeśa*

The same thing may have value and fault;
the same river water that tastes sweet
turns undrinkable in the sea.
— *Hitopadeśa*

Friendships with the crass are like clay pots;
easily shattered any day, and hard to join again.
Friendships with good men on the other hand,
are like cups of gold;
hard to spoil or splinter, and
quick to mend or mould.
— *Hitopadeśa*

To the contented one, all of earth is spread with fine leather when he has shoes on his feet. The world's riches are yours if your heart is contented.
— *Hitopadeśa*

Whether drinking water or alcohol,
in contentment lies happiness.
— *Hitopadeśa* (Adapted)

If a man does not seek his master's fall let me speak frankly; this is his duty and any other course is contrary to the law.
— *Hitopadeśa*

Princes trust those who don't carry on intrigues
with the royal harem's attendants.
Or whisper to the king's advisers
— *Hitopadeśa*

How can a mind find tranquility
if his home is at the sea's edge,
if his wife sleeps with another man
or if his home is haunted by snakes.
— *Hitopadeśa*

For most of us it is hard to figure out our ability.
If we could judge that with clarity,
it would save us a lot of misery.
— *Hitopadeśa*

A coward does not start on a new venture because he fears failure. Should one not eat because he fears a stomach ache.
— *Hitopadeśa*

Horses and elephants follow orders.
Animals understand when instructed.
But the clever infer even what is unsaid
and know what appeals to others.

— Hitopadeśa

When kings and armies lie dead in a battlefield
vultures and other scavengers don't lose a moment
to decide on sharing the spoils.

— Hitopadeśa

Match your words with the occasion.
Match your courtesies with your intention.
Match your anger with deeds.

— Hitopadeśa

Whatever pleases us has beauty in our eyes.
There is nothing ugly or beautiful by nature.

— Hitopadeśa

Just as two logs meet by chance
and drift away in the river's vista,
we will meet and part in life's expanse.

— Hitopadeśa

Our body disintegrates into five elements on death.
Each goes back to its own source and is absorbed.
Why then do we mourn?

— Hitopadeśa

As many times as you form relationships
that bring you happiness and pleasure
an equal number of times,
sorrow's dart pierces deep inside your heart.
— *Hitopadeśa*

When there is no chance
that we will be with our own body forever,
why hope that we will be with somebody eternally.
— *Hitopadeśa*

A messenger will not lie
even when weapons are pointed at him.
Asked to deliver the message, he is certain to tell the truth.
— *Hitopadeśa*

Getting into a fight when the time is not right
is just like a crow trying to fly at night.
But timing your moves after seeing an opportunity
is akin to an owl who can see even through darkness
— *Hitopadeśa*

The greatest gift is security,
not land or gold or food.
— *Hitopadeśa*

Life is like a fleeting moon's reflection on water.
If you appreciate that, spend it doing good deeds.
— *Hitopadeśa*

The ignorant commit illegal acts
for the sake of material comfort and wealth.
Most of which are perishable or transitory at best.

— *Panchtantra*

The weight of apples bends the apple tree low.
The plumage slows the peacock's walk.
The blue blooded race horse is led like a cow.
In those endowed by great qualities,
those very qualities become their biggest drawbacks.

— *Panchtantra*

Self examination is not easy. Either we don't know how to or don't have the humility to review our actions. But if we do undertake self examination, even the worst blows won't sink us.

— *Panchtantra*

There is no greater penance than patience;
no greater joy than contentment;
no greater giving than friendship;
no greater virtue than compassion.

— *Panchtantra*

The ignorant hate the wise.
The poor hate the wealthy.
The corrupt hate the honest.
Women of loose character hate devoted wives.

— *Panchtantra*

Wounds become vulnerable to new infections.
Lack of food makes a man forget everything else.
New problems seem to crop up in a bad situation.
Misfortunes tend to add up at the weakest points.
— *Panchtantra*

The first mark of intelligence is to leave well alone
things that are going well.
The second mark of intelligence
is to take what you begin to its logical conclusion.
— *Panchtantra*

Sources

Hitopadeśa

Literally, "Teachings on Well Being" the *Hitopadeśa* is a collection of fables in prose and verse that impart knowledge on governance and strategy. The ancient Indian text uses the art of story-telling to teach through examples. The pattern is to weave a story within a story.

The story goes that a king was worried that his sons were not learning. He assigned the task to Vişnu Şarma, who then set about teaching the princes through the stories of *Hitopadeśa*.

Panchtantra

The *Panchtantra*, also by Vişnu Şarma, is a repository of the central Hindu principles of Nīti, or wise conduct. This work, too, uses the art of story-telling, with all the stories strung together like pearls on a string.

The goal was to teach the princes how to think rather than what to think.

Arthaśāstra

Literally, "The Book of Wealth" or "The Book of Economics." Written by Kautilya (Chanakya), it is also a book of political strategy, and is often thought to bear a strikingly parallel to Machiavelli's *The Prince.*

Chanakya (Kautilya)

Chanakya (350-275 BCE) was an Indian teacher, philosopher, economist, jurist and royal adviser. He is traditionally identified as Kautilya or Vishnu Gupta, who authored the *Arthaśāstra*, the seminal Indian treatise on political science and economics.

Chanakya taught at the ancient university of Takshashila, and later proved himself to be a master strategist who is widely credited for having played an important role in the establishment of the considerable Maurya Empire in India.

Sutta Pitaka

Consisting of more than 10,000 sermons, *Sutta Pitaka,* "The Basket of Discourses," is the oldest record of what are believed to be the discourses delivered by the Buddha and his chief disciples.